D1490522

Enterprise Analytics

Enterprise Analytics

Optimize Performance, Process, and Decisions Through Big Data

Thomas H. Davenport

Vice President, Publisher: Tim Moore
Associate Publisher and Director of Marketing: Amy Neidlinger
Executive Editor: Jeanne Glasser Levine
Editorial Assistant: Pamela Boland
Operations Specialist: Jodi Kemper
Marketing Manager: Megan Graue
Cover Designer: Chuti Prasertsith
Managing Editor: Kristy Hart
Senior Project Editor: Lori Lyons
Copy Editor: Gayle Johnson
Proofreader: Chrissy White, Language Logistics, LLC
Indexer: Cheryl Lenser
Compositor: Nonie Ratcliff
Manufacturing Buyer: Dan Uhrig

© 2013 by International Institute for Analytics
Pearson Education, Inc.
Publishing as FT Press
Upper Saddle River, New Jersey 07458

This book is sold with the understanding that neither the author nor the publisher is engaged in rendering legal, accounting, or other professional services or advice by publishing this book. Each individual situation is unique. Thus, if legal or financial advice or other expert assistance is required in a specific situation, the services of a competent professional should be sought to ensure that the situation has been evaluated carefully and appropriately. The author and the publisher disclaim any liability, loss, or risk resulting directly or indirectly, from the use or application of any of the contents of this book.

FT Press offers excellent discounts on this book when ordered in quantity for bulk purchases or special sales. For more information, please contact U.S. Corporate and Government Sales, 1-800-382-3419, corpsales@pearsontechgroup.com. For sales outside the U.S., please contact International Sales at international@pearsoned.com.

Company and product names mentioned herein are the trademarks or registered trademarks of their respective owners.

All rights reserved. No part of this book may be reproduced, in any form or by any means, without permission in writing from the publisher.

Printed in the United States of America

Third Printing April 2013

ISBN-10: 0-13-303943-9
ISBN-13: 978-0-13-303943-6

Pearson Education LTD.
Pearson Education Australia PTY, Limited.
Pearson Education Singapore, Pte. Ltd.
Pearson Education Asia, Ltd.
Pearson Education Canada, Ltd.
Pearson Educación de Mexico, S.A. de C.V.
Pearson Education—Japan
Pearson Education Malaysia, Pte. Ltd.

Library of Congress Cataloging-in-Publication Data

Enterprise analytics : optimize performance, process, and decisions through big data / [edited by] Thomas H. Davenport.
    p. cm.
  ISBN 978-0-13-303943-6 (hardcover : alk. paper)
  1. Business intelligence. 2. Decision making. 3. Management. I. Davenport, Thomas H., 1954-
  HD38.7.E557 2013
  658.4'038--dc23
                                2012024235

Contents at a Glance

Contents

Foreword and Acknowledgments

The collection of research in this book personifies the contributions of a group of people who have made the International Institute for Analytics the success it is today. This book is the result of three cups of hard work, two cups of perseverance, and a pinch of serendipity that got our fledgling company started.

First, the hard work. Obvious thanks go to Tom Davenport for editing and compiling this initial collection of IIA research into book form. For the raw material Tom had to work with, thanks to all IIA faculty members who have contributed insightful research during IIA's first two years, particularly Bill Franks, Jeanne Harris, Bob Morison, James Taylor, Eric Peterson, and Keri Pearlson. Marcia Testa (Harvard School of Public Health) and Dwight McNeil played key roles as we grew our coverage of health care analytics. Ananth Raman (Harvard Business School) and Marshall Fisher (Wharton) were instrumental in forming our initial retail analytics research agenda. We look forward to additional books in these two areas. And, of course, thanks to all the practitioner organizations who volunteered their time to be the subjects of much of our research.

For their continued belief in IIA, thanks to the entire team at SAS, who validated our mission and direction early on and have shown their trust in us ever since. In particular, thanks to Scott Van Valkenburgh (for all the whiteboard sessions), Deb Orton, Mike Bright, Anne Milley, and Adele Sweetwood. We're also grateful for the support of other IIA underwriters, including Accenture, Dell, Intel, SAP, and Teradata.

This book is also a credit to the perseverance of two great talents within IIA. Katherine Busey was IIA's first employee in Boston and was the person who helped convince Jeanne Glasser at Pearson that IIA's research deserved to be read by more than just our research clients. Thanks as well to Callie Youssi, who coordinates all of IIA's faculty research activities, which is no simple task.

It's hard to imagine Tom without his wife and agent, Jodi, to add vector to the thrust. Thanks to you both for betting on me as an entrepreneur, particularly during a challenging first year.

And for the pinch of serendipity, Tom and I are indebted to Eric McNulty for having the foresight to bring us together, be the first voice of IIA, and help set our early publishing and research standards.

Jack Phillips
Chief Executive Officer, International Institute for Analytics

About the Authors

Thomas H. Davenport is co-founder and research director of IIA, a Visiting Professor at Harvard Business School, Distinguished Professor at Babson College, and a Senior Advisor to Deloitte Analytics. Voted the third leading business-strategy analyst (just behind Peter Drucker and Tom Friedman) in *Optimize* magazine, Davenport is a world-renowned thought leader who has helped hundreds of companies revitalize their management practices. His Competing on Analytics idea recently was named by *Harvard Business Review* one of the 12 most important management ideas of the past decade. The related article was named one of the ten must-read articles in *HBR*'s 75-year history. Published in February 2010, Davenport's related book, *Analytics at Work: Smarter Decisions, Better Results*, was named one of the top 15 must-reads for 2010 by *CIO Insight*.

Elizabeth Craig is a research fellow with the Accenture Institute for High Performance in Boston. She is the coauthor, with Peter Cheese and Robert J. Thomas, of *The Talent-Powered Organization* (Kogan Page, 2007).

Jeanne G. Harris is a senior executive research fellow with the Accenture Institute for High Performance in Chicago. She is coauthor, with Thomas H. Davenport and Robert Morison, of *Analytics at Work: Smarter Decisions, Better Results* (Harvard Business Press, 2010). She also cowrote the 2007 book *Competing on Analytics: The New Science of Winning* (also from Harvard Business Press).

Robert Morison serves as lead faculty for the Enterprise Research Subscription of IIA. He is an accomplished business researcher, writer, discussion leader, and management consultant. He is coauthor of *Analytics at Work: Smarter Decisions, Better Results* (Harvard Business Press, 2010), *Workforce Crisis: How to Beat the Coming Shortage of Skills and Talent* (Harvard Business Press, 2006), and three *Harvard Business Review* articles, one of which received a McKinsey Award as best article of 2004. He has spoken before scores of corporate, industry, and government groups and has been a commentator on workforce issues on *Nightly Business Report* on PBS. Most recently executive vice president and director of research with nGenera Corporation, he earlier held management positions with the Concours Group, CSC Index, and General Electric Information Services Company.

Dr. Keri E. Pearlson is an expert in the area of managing and using information. She has worked with CIOs and executives from some of the largest corporations in the world. She has expertise in helping executives create strategies to become Web 2.0-enabled enterprises, designing and delivering executive leadership programs, and managing multiclient programs on issues of interest to senior executives of information systems. She specializes in helping IT executives prepare to participate in the strategy formulation processes with their executive peers. She's a faculty member of the International Institute for Analytics and the Founding Partner and President of KP Partners, a CIO advisory services firm.

Bill Franks is a faculty member of the International Institute for Analytics and is Chief Analytics Officer for Teradata's global alliance programs. He also oversees the Business Analytic Innovation Center, which is jointly sponsored by Teradata and SAS; it focuses on helping clients pursue innovative analytics. In addition, Bill works to help determine the right strategies and positioning for Teradata in the advanced analytics space. He is the author of the book *Taming the Big Data Tidal Wave* (John Wiley & Sons, Inc., April, 2012, www.tamingthebigdatatidalwave.com).

Eric T. Peterson is a faculty member of the International Institute for Analytics. He is the founder of Web Analytics Demystified and has worked in web analytics for over 10 years as a practitioner, consultant, and analyst. He is the author of three best-selling web analytics books: *Web Analytics Demystified*, *Web Site Measurement Hacks*, and *The Big Book of Key Performance Indicators*. He is one of the most widely read web analytics writers at www.webanalyticsdemystified.com.

John Lucker is a principal with Deloitte Consulting LLP, where he leads Deloitte's Advanced Analytics and Modeling practice, one of the leading analytics groups in the professional services industry. He has vast experience in the areas of advanced analytics, predictive modeling, data mining, scoring and rules engines, and numerous other advanced analytics business solution approaches.

James Taylor is a faculty member of the International Institute for Analytics and is CEO of Decision Management Solutions. Decision Management Systems apply business rules, predictive analytics, and optimization technologies to address the toughest issues facing businesses today, changing how organizations do business. He has over 20 years of experience in developing software and solutions for clients. He has led Decision Management efforts for leading companies in insurance, banking, health management, and telecommunications.

Stacy Blanchard is the Organization Effectiveness Services and Human Capital Analytics lead for Accenture Analytics. With over 15 years of experience in aligning strategy, culture, and leadership for organizations, she has worked globally across a multitude of client situations and industries. She integrates real-world experience with recognized approaches to coach and align the C-suite to drive transformational agendas. Prior to Accenture, she was the CEO of Hagberg Consulting Group, an organization consultancy specializing in the assessment, alignment, and transformation of strategy, corporate culture, and leadership.

Carl Schleyer is Director of Operations and Analytics for Sears Holdings Corporation (an IIA sponsor) and is responsible for gathering and analyzing large volumes of data in order to support talent and human capital strategies and tactics. As a part of this role, Carl created the first analytical team dedicated to purely human capital pursuits within Sears Holdings. His passion is unlocking the value of data through influencing decisions. Carl is a 20+ year veteran of the retail industry, having served various functions within HR.

Leandro DalleMule is Senior Director for Global Analytics at CitiGroup. Prior to this, he was a Senior Manager for Deloitte's analytics consulting practice, a risk manager for GE Capital, and a brand manager for Exxon in Brazil.

Callie Youssi is Vice President of Research Operations for the International Institute for Analytics. In this role, she works to build, manage, and support IIA's global faculty as they uncover the most compelling applications of analytics. She is responsible for aggregating and analyzing the areas of greatest interest to IIA clients and ensuring a strong faculty bench to address those focus areas.

Katherine Busey is Vice President of Business Development for the International Institute for Analytics. In this role, she is responsible for developing global business opportunities for IIA. She works with IIA's underwriters, partners, and research clients to uncover new trends in the analytics space and bring together vendors and practitioners.

Introduction: The New World of Enterprise Analytics

Thomas H. Davenport

The Rise of Analytics

Analytics aren't new—I've found references to corporate analytical groups as far back as 1954—but they seem to be more important to business and organizational life than ever before. Analytical approaches to decision-making and management are on the rise because of several factors:

- The dramatic increase in the amounts of data to analyze from various business information systems
- Powerful and inexpensive computers and software that can analyze all this data
- The movement of quantitatively trained managers into positions of responsibility within organizations
- The need to differentiate products and offers, optimize prices and inventories, and understand what drives various aspects of business performance

As a result, many factors indicate that analytical initiatives, jobs, and organizations are taking off around the world. According to LinkedIn data, for example, the number of people starting analytics or data scientist jobs increased tenfold from 1990 to 2010. Every major consulting firm has developed an analytics practice. According to Google Trends, the number of searches using the term "analytics" increased more than twenty-fold between 2005 and 2012; searches for the term "big data" (defined in a moment) showed an even more dramatic rise beginning in 2010. The current era has been described as the "Age of Analytics," the "Age of Algorithms," and the "Money-ball Era," after the book and movie about the application of analytics to professional baseball.

Enterprise Analytics

One important attribute of the increased focus on analytics is that it has become—at least for many organizations—an "enterprise" resource. That is, instead of being sequestered into several small pockets of an organization—market research or actuarial or quality management—analytical capabilities are being recognized as some-thing that can benefit an entire organization. Diverse groups are being centralized, or at least coordination and communication are taking place between them. Analytical talent is being inventoried and assessed across the organization. Plans, initiatives, and priorities are being determined by enterprise-level groups, and the goal is to maxi-mize the impact on the enterprise.

Hence the title of this book. Many of the chapters relate to how analytics can and should be managed at an enterprise level. If there were a set of guidelines for a Chief Analytics Officer—and some peo-ple in this role are emerging, albeit still in relatively small numbers—this book would provide many of them. We are not yet at the point where analytics is a broadly recognized business function, but we are clearly moving in that direction.

The Rise of "Big Data"

Excitement about analytics has been augmented by even more excitement about *big data*. The concept refers to data that is either too voluminous or too unstructured to be managed and analyzed through traditional means. The definition is clearly a relative one that will change over time. Currently, "too voluminous" typically means databases or data flows in petabytes (1,000 terabytes); Google, for example, processes about 24 petabytes of data per day. "Too unstructured" generally means that the data isn't easily put into the traditional rows and columns of conventional databases.

Examples of big data include a massive amount of online information, including clickstream data from the Web and social media content (tweets, blogs, wall postings). Big data also incorporates video data from retail and crime/intelligence environments, or rendering of video entertainment. It includes voice data from call centers and intelligence interventions. In the life sciences, it includes genomic and proteomic data from biological research and medicine.

Many IT vendors and solutions providers, and some of their customers, treat the term as just another buzzword for analytics, or for managing and analyzing data to better understand the business. But there is more than vendor hype; there are considerable business benefits from being able to analyze big data on a consistent basis.

Companies that excel at big data will be able to use other new technologies, such as ubiquitous sensors and the "Internet of things." Virtually every mechanical or electronic device can leave a trail that describes its performance, location, or state. These devices, and the people who use them, communicate through the Internet—which leads to another vast data source. When all these bits are combined with those from other media—wireless and wired telephony, cable, satellite, and so forth—the future of data appears even bigger.

Companies that employ these tools will ultimately be able to understand their business environment at the most granular level and adapt to it rapidly. They'll be able to differentiate commodity products and services by monitoring and analyzing usage patterns. And in the life sciences, of course, effective use of big data can yield cures to the most threatening diseases.

Big data and analytics based on it promise to change virtually every industry and business function over the next decade. Organizations that get started early with big data can gain a significant competitive edge. Just as early analytical competitors in the "small data" era (including Capital One bank, Progressive insurance, and Marriott hotels) moved out ahead of their competitors and built a sizable competitive edge, the time is now for firms to seize the big-data opportunity.

The availability of all this data means that virtually every business or organizational activity can be viewed as a big-data problem or initiative. Manufacturing, in which most machines already have one or more microprocessors, is already a big-data situation. Consumer marketing, with myriad customer touchpoints and clickstreams, is already a big-data problem. Governments have begun to recognize that they sit on enormous collections of data that wait to be analyzed. Google has even described the self-driving car as a big data problem.

This book is based primarily on small-data analytics, but occasionally it refers to big data, data scientists, and other issues related to the topic. Certainly many of the ideas from traditional analytics are highly relevant to big-data analytics as well.

IIA and the Research for This Book

I have been doing research on analytics for the last fifteen years or so. In 2010 Jack Phillips, an information industry entrepreneur, and I cofounded the International Institute for Analytics (IIA). This still-young organization was launched as a research and advisory service for vendors and users of analytics and analytical technologies. I had previously led sponsored research programs on analytics, and I knew they were a great way to generate relevant research content.

The earliest support for the Institute came from the leading analytics vendor SAS. We also worked with key partners of SAS, including Intel, Accenture, and Teradata. A bit later, other key vendors, including SAP and Dell, became sponsors of IIA. The sponsors of IIA provided not only financial support for the research, but also researchers and thought leaders in analytics who served as IIA faculty.

After recruiting other faculty with academic or independent consulting backgrounds, we began producing research outputs. You'll see several examples of the research outputs in this book. The IIA produced three types of outputs: research briefs (typically three-to-five-page documents on particular analytics topics); leading-practice briefs (case studies on firms with leading or typical analytical issues);

and write-ups of meetings, webcasts, and audioconferences. The emphasis was on short, digestible documents, although in some cases more than one brief or document has been combined to make one chapter in this book.

With some initial research in hand, we began recruiting corporate or organizational participants in IIA. Our initial approach was to focus on general "enterprise" topics—how to organize analytics, technology architectures for analytics, and so forth. We did find a good reaction to these topics, many of which are covered in this book. Practitioner companies and individual members began to join IIA in substantial numbers.

However, the strongest response was to our idea for industry-specific research. Companies seemed quite interested in general materials about analytical best practices but were even more interested in how to employ analytics in health care or retail, our first two industry-specific programs. That research is not featured in this book—we may do other books on analytics within specific industries—but we did include some of the leading-practice briefs from those industries as chapters.

The Structure of This Book

All the chapters in this book were produced in or derived from IIA projects. All the authors (or at least one author of each chapter) are IIA faculty members. A few topics have appeared in a similar (but not exactly the same) form in journal articles or books, but most have not been published outside of IIA. The chapters describe several broad topics. Part I is an overview of analytics and its value. Part II discusses applying analytics. Part III covers technologies for analytics. Part IV describes the human side of analytics. Part V consists of case studies of analytical activity within organizations.

Part I
Overview of Analytics and Their Value

1

What Do We Talk About When We Talk About Analytics?

Thomas H. Davenport

Every decade or so, the business world invents another term for how it extracts managerial and decision-making value from computerized data. In the 1970s the favored term was *decision support systems*, accurately reflecting the importance of a decision-centered approach to data analysis. In the early '80s, *executive information systems* was the preferred nomenclature, which addressed the use of these systems by senior managers. Later in that decade, emphasis shifted to the more technical-sounding *online analytical processing* (OLAP). The '90s saw the rise of *business intelligence* as a descriptor.

Each of these terms has its virtues and its ambiguities. No supreme being has provided us with a clear, concise definition of what anything should be called, so we mortals will continue to wrestle with appropriate terminology. It appears, however, that another shift is taking place in the label for how we take advantage of data to make better decisions and manage organizations. The new label is *analytics*, which began to come into favor in the middle of this century's first decade—at least for the more statistical and mathematical forms of data analysis.

Jeanne Harris, my coauthor on the 2007 book *Competing on Analytics*, and I defined analytics as "the extensive use of data, statistical and quantitative analysis, explanatory and predictive models, and fact-based management to drive decisions and actions." I still like that definition, although now I would have to admit that they are still analytics even if they don't drive decisions and actions. If a tree falls in the woods and nobody chops it up for firewood, it's still a tree.

Of course, no term stays static after it is introduced into the marketplace. It evolves and accretes new meanings over time. Particularly if it is a popular term, technology vendors claim that their product or service is at least a piece of the term, and they often represent it as being squarely in the center of the term's definition. That is certainly the case with analytics. The term also has many commonly used variations:

- Predictive analytics
- Data mining
- Business analytics
- Web analytics
- Big-data analytics

I'll attempt to shed more light on how the term *analytics* has evolved and the meanings of some of the key variations as well. Before doing that, however, I should remind you that analytics aren't a new idea, and they don't have to be tied up with analytical technology. The first writing on statistics was arguably by Al-Kindi, an Arab philosopher from the 9th century. It is believed that he possessed rather primitive computing tools. Even today, theoretically, analytics could be carried out using paper, pencil, and perhaps a slide rule, but it would be foolish not to employ computers and software. If you own a copy of Microsoft Excel, for example, you have the ability to do fairly sophisticated statistical analyses on lots of data. And today the vendors of analytical software range from open-source statistics-oriented programming languages (R, Julia) to specialized analytics firms (Minitab, Stata, and the much-larger firm SAS) to IT giants such as IBM, SAP, and Oracle. Because they involve data and computers, analytics also require good information management capabilities to clean, integrate, extract, transform, and access data. It might be tempting, then, to simply equate analytics with analytical information technology. But this would be a mistake, since it's the human and organizational aspects of analytics that are often most difficult and truly differentiating.

Why We Needed a New Term: Issues with Traditional Business Intelligence

Business intelligence (BI) used to be primarily about generating standard reports or answering queries, although many viewed it as incorporating more analytical activities as well. Today it has come to stand for a variety of diverse activities. The Wikipedia definition of BI (as of April 10, 2012), for example, is rather extended:

> Business intelligence (BI) mainly refers to computer-based techniques used in identifying, extracting, and analyzing business data, such as sales revenue by products and/or departments, or by associated costs and incomes.

> BI technologies provide historical, current and predictive views of business operations. Common functions of business intelligence technologies are reporting, online analytical processing, analytics, data mining, process mining, complex event processing, business performance management, benchmarking, text mining and predictive analytics.

> Business intelligence aims to support better business decision-making. Thus a BI system can be called a decision support system (DSS). Though the term business intelligence is sometimes used as a synonym for competitive intelligence, because they both support decision making, BI uses technologies, processes, and applications to analyze mostly internal, structured data and business processes while competitive intelligence gathers, analyzes and disseminates information with a topical focus on company competitors. Business intelligence understood broadly can include the subset of competitive intelligence.

You know there is a problem when a definition requires that much verbiage! BI has always had its issues as a term. While surely preferable to "business stupidity," it lacked precision as to what activities were included. One business school faculty colleague of mine suggested that it was highly presumptuous for the IT field to claim "business intelligence" as its own. Aren't all business activities supposed to add intelligence? And how does business intelligence relate to such fields as competitive intelligence (which is described as a subset of business intelligence in the Wikipedia definition, but tends not to involve much quantified data at all) and customer intelligence?

The problems of BI multiplied when the term *analytics* began to gain favor around the middle of the last decade. There was much confusion about the difference between these two terms. The CEO of a software vendor in this category told me he thought that analytics was a subset of business intelligence. Another CEO in the same industry argued that BI was a subset of analytics. Obviously neither term is entirely clear if each can be a subset of the other in educated executives' minds.

There is little doubt, however, that analytics have become a more contemporary synonym for business intelligence, but with a more quantitatively sophisticated slant. The reporting-oriented activities that primarily characterized BI are now considered a part of analytics by many people and organizations. However, it's fair to say that every form of analytics is in some sense a struggle between the reporting-centric activities common in business intelligence and the more sophisticated analytical approaches involving statistics and mathematical models of data. Therefore, it's important to be clear about the different types of activities that are possible under the banner of "analytics."

Three Types of Analytics

If the term *analytics* is to retain any real meaning with so much evolution in the term, we probably require some subdefinitions of analytics. For example, if we include the various forms of reporting—standard or ad hoc reports, queries, scorecards, alerts—in analytics, perhaps they should be called *descriptive analytics* (see Figure 1.1). They simply describe what has happened in the past. Descriptive analytics may also be used to classify customers or other business entities into groups that are similar on certain dimensions.

It would be difficult to argue that understanding what has happened is not a good thing for organizations to do. What could be objectionable about it? Nothing, really, except that there are more sophisticated ways of using data to understand a business. Your statistics textbook didn't end with means, medians, and modes, and you can go beyond descriptive analytics. The numbers from descriptive analytics don't tell you anything about the future, they don't tell you anything about what the numbers should be, and they usually don't tell you much about why they are what they are.

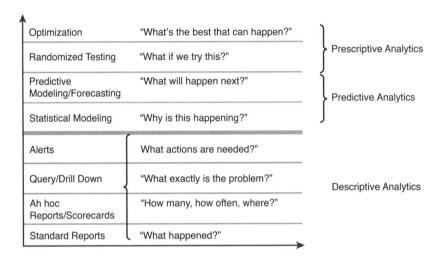

Figure 1.1 Three types of business analytics.

Predictive analytics use models of the past to predict the future. They typically use multiple variables to predict a particular dependent variable. Examples include using various measures of growing season rainfall and temperatures to predict the price of Bordeaux wine, or using variables about your credit history to predict the likelihood that you will repay loans in the future. Predictive analytics models are very popular in predicting the behavior of customers based on past buying history and perhaps some demographic variables.

Note that incorporated into the predictive analytics category in Figure 1.1 is statistical modeling. Technically this type of analysis is still about explaining—rather than predicting—what happens in an organization. However, it is a necessary step in predictive analytics. You can't project a model into the future unless you start with a good model fitting past data. Once you do have a model, you can plug in various estimates of what your independent variables might be and come out with a prediction for your dependent variable.

Prescriptive analytics are less widely known, but I refer to them as prescriptive because, in effect, they tell you what to do. Randomized testing, in which a test group is compared to a control group with random assignment of subjects to each group, is a powerful method to establish cause. If you compare the two groups and find that one is better than the other with statistical significance, you should do the thing that's being tested in the test group.

Optimization is another form of prescriptive analytics. It tells you, based on a statistical model, what the optimum level of key variables is if you want to maximize a particular outcome variable. If you want to maximize your profitability, for example, pricing optimization tells you what price to charge for your products and services.

Each of these three types of analytics is valuable, but in most organizations, descriptive analytics dominate in terms of frequency of use. Reporting tools are widely available and easy to understand. Managers often demand them, as do external regulatory bodies. Therefore, they tend to become so common that they drive out more sophisticated analytics. Companies that want to emphasize predictive and prescriptive analytics sometimes have to control the demand and supply for descriptive analytics. One way to do this is by encouraging managers to do their own query and reporting work, rather than have quantitative analysts do it for them.

Where Does Data Mining Fit In?

Data mining can fit into any of the three categories just described, but it most commonly involves statistical and predictive models—predictive analytics in Figure 1.1. The Wikipedia definition (as of April 12, 2012) starts with the following:

> Data mining (the analysis step of the knowledge discovery in databases process, or KDD), a relatively young and interdisciplinary field of computer science, is the process of discovering new patterns from large data sets involving methods at the intersection of artificial intelligence, machine learning, statistics and database systems.

As this definition suggests, data mining implies a discovery of trends and patterns in data—not by humans, but by the computer itself. Artificial intelligence (notably, neural networks) and machine learning approaches rely on computers and software to try a variety of models to fit the data and determine the optimal model. Traditional analytics rely on a human analyst to generate a hypothesis and test it with a model.

Data mining implies a lesser need for smart humans, but this is not the case in the companies I have studied. In fact, every company I have seen with an aggressive data mining initiative also has a large complement of sophisticated quantitative people. It is true that machine learning can increase the productivity of those smart humans, but they are still necessary to configure the machine learning programs, tune them, and interpret the results. In big data environments, machine learning is often necessary to create models for the vast and continuing amount of data; human analysts using hypothesis-driven analytics alone just can't keep up.

Business Analytics Versus Other Types

Over the past several years, the term *business analytics* has become popular. It merely means using analytics in business to improve business performance and better satisfy customers.

Analytics are also being applied in other nonbusiness sectors, such as health care and life sciences, education, and government. Some of these areas have particular names for their approaches to analytics. In health care, for example, the use of the term *health care analytics* is growing in popularity, and you also are likely to hear *informatics* and *clinical decision support* used as synonyms.

Each industry and sector has its own orientations to analytics. Even what is called "health care analytics" or "clinical decision support" in health care is somewhat dissimilar to analytics in other industries. It is likely, for example, that the primary method for supporting decisions in health care will be a series of if/then rules, rather than statistical models or algorithms—although there is slow movement toward more quantitative data.

Web Analytics

Web analytics is about analyzing online activity on websites and in web applications. Perhaps obviously, it is one of the newer analytical disciplines. And perhaps because of its youth, it is relatively immature and rapidly changing. For most organizations, web analytics is really web reporting—counting how many unique visitors have come to the site, how many pages they have viewed, how long they have stayed. Knowing these details is certainly valuable, but at some point perhaps web analytics will commonly employ more sophisticated analyses. As Brent Dykes puts it in the fun book *Web Analytics Action Hero*, if all you do is count things, you will forever be stuck in "Setupland" as opposed to becoming an action hero.

The great exception to the web analytics = web reporting equation is the use of prescriptive analytics in the form of randomized testing, often called *A/B testing* in web analytics. This involves testing two different versions of a web page, typically to learn which receives more traffic. Customers or users of the website need not even know they are participating in a test. More sophisticated testing is sometimes done using multiple variables and even testing across multiple channels (a website plus a print ad, for example).

Highly analytical companies such as Google and eBay typically run hundreds or thousands of tests at once. They have millions of customers, so it is relatively easy to create test and control groups and serve them different pages. eBay has an advanced testing platform that makes it easy for different groups within the company to run and interpret tests. However, there is still the issue of ensuring that the same customer is not participating in too many tests—participating in one test may confound the results from another—and determining for how long the learnings from a test remain relevant.

Big-Data Analytics

The newest forms of analytics are related to *big data*. This term usually refers to data that is either too big, too unstructured, or from too many different sources to be manageable through traditional databases. It is often encountered in online environments such as text, images, and video on websites. Scientific data, such as genomic data in biology, also usually falls into the big-data category in terms of both volume and (lack of) structure.

As Bill Franks of Teradata pointed out in an IIA blog post, "the fact is that virtually no analytics directly analyze unstructured data. Unstructured data may be an input to an analytic process, but when it comes time to do any actual analysis, the unstructured data itself isn't utilized." He goes on to say that in almost all cases, unstructured data—text, images, whatever—needs to be converted into structured and usually quantitative data before it is analyzed. That's what increasingly popular tools such as Hadoop and MapReduce do— "preprocess" data in various ways to turn it into structured, quantitative data that can be analyzed. For example, a company might be interested in understanding online consumer sentiment about the company or its brands. They might take text from blog posts, Twitter tweets, and discussion boards that mention the company as the input to an analysis. But before it can be analyzed, they need to classify the language in the text as either positive, negative, or neutral. The analysis typically just averages the resulting numbers (typically 1, 0, or –1).

Unfortunately, that relatively simple level of analysis is all too common in big-data analytics. The data management work needed to wrestle big data into shape for analysis is often quite sophisticated and demanding. But, as in web analytics, the actual analysis techniques used on the data are often underwhelming. There is a lot of counting and reporting of categories, as well as visual representations of those counts and reports. There is very little predictive or prescriptive analytics performed on big data.

Perhaps this will change over time as the data management activities around big data become more routine and less labor-intensive. Certainly many of the "data scientists" who work with big data have highly quantitative backgrounds. PhDs in scientific or mathematics/statistics abound in this job category. These people presumably would be capable of much more sophisticated analyses. But at the moment their analytical skills are being tested far less than their data management skills.

Conclusion

What's in a name? Using the term *analytics* instead of prior terms may help inspire organizations to use more sophisticated mathematical and statistical decision tools for business problem-solving and competitive advantage. Just as the term *supply chain management* created a sense of process and interdependence that was not conveyed by "shipping," a new term for the widespread analysis of data for decision-making purposes may assist in transforming that function. We live in a world in which many amazing feats of data manipulation and algorithmic transformation are possible. The name for these activities might as well reflect their power and potential.

One risk with the field of analytics, however, is that too much gets wrapped into the name. If analytics becomes totally synonymous with business intelligence or decision support—and the great majority of the activities underneath the term involve simple counting and reporting—the term, and the field it describes, will lose a lot of its power. Organizations wanting to ensure that analytics is more than just reporting should be sure to discriminate among the different types of analytics in the terminology they employ.

2

The Return on Investments in Analytics

Keri E. Pearlson

Deciding to invest in an analytics project and then evaluating the success of that investment are complex processes. Often the decision is complicated by the complexity of the project, the time lag between the investment and the realization of benefits, and the difficulty in identifying the actual costs and actual value. However, most go/no-go decisions are made on the basis of a calculation of the return on investment (ROI), through either a formal ROI calculation or an informal assessment of the answer to the question "Will the value be greater than the investment?" The objective of this chapter is to summarize the traditional approaches to calculating ROI and then to describe a particular approach to ROI analysis used by Teradata, a provider of technologies and services including data warehousing, BI, and customer relationship management (CRM). I'll conclude with a case study on the business justification of analytics at the semiconductor firm Freescale.

Traditional ROI Analysis

The concept of calculating the ROI is simple, but the actual process to do so can be complicated. Despite this difficulty, ROI is useful in making the business case for the initial investment and also is used after the fact to evaluate the investment. We'll begin this chapter by looking at the traditional method of calculating ROI and some of the considerations you face when doing so for investments in analytics.

A traditional ROI would have the analyst calculate a simple equation:

$$ROI = \frac{\text{Total value / benefits} - \text{Total investment costs}}{\text{Total investment costs}}$$

When it is part of the business case, this calculation is used in two ways. First, if the result of this simple calculation is a positive number, that means the cost of the investment is less than the value received. Therefore, the investment has a positive return and is potentially a "good" investment. Likewise, if it is a negative number, it is not a good investment. The second way this calculation is used is to compare investment opportunities. ROI calculations typically are expressed as this ratio to normalize the result and provide a basis for comparison with other investment opportunities. In many organizations, this ratio must exceed a minimum level to be considered for funding in resource allocation decisions.

Let's consider a simple example. Suppose a retail company is evaluating the potential return on the investment of an analytics project aimed at producing a more successful direct-mail campaign. The company plans to build a model of high-potential customers based on criteria selection and then mine its CRM data for these customers. Instead of sending a mailing to all customers who have spent $500 in the past year, the company will send the mailing only to customers who meet a selection of additional criteria. To build and run the model, the investment in the analytics project will cost $50,000. The expected benefit is calculated at $75,000 (you'll read more about how this might be calculated later). Plugging these numbers into the ROI formula yields this equation:

$$ROI = \frac{\$75,000 - \$50,000}{\$50,000} = \frac{\$25,000}{\$50,000} = 50\%$$

Clearly, if a second project cost $100,000 and the expected benefit were $130,000, the ROI would be 30%.

What would we do with these ROI numbers? First, if budget permits, we might make both investments, given both are projected to return more than they cost (we know this because the ROI is positive). Alternatively, the internal budget policy might be to invest only in projects with at least a 40% return. Therefore, the first investment passed this hurdle, but the second one did not.

If we can make only one investment (perhaps the resources or the people needed to do these projects are the same and cannot do both at the same time), we could compare the investments to each other. A return of 50% is more than a return of 30%, so we might be more inclined to make the first investment. But at the same time, the actual benefit from the first investment is much less than the actual benefit from the second investment ($75,000 versus $150,000), supporting a decision to make the second investment. Given these calculations, it would take a budget committee or decision-maker to make the actual decision.

Cash Flow and ROI

In this simple example, the assumption is that the costs and benefits occur at the same time. That is rarely the case with an actual analytics project (or any business project). The ROI calculation must result from a realistic cash flow over the period of the project with the timing in mind. It's beyond the scope of this chapter to explain this type of complex ROI calculation, but some websites have good examples, such as http://bit.ly/IIACashFlow.

Building a Credible ROI

A credible ROI is based on a credible business case. Expected benefits must clearly be a result of the investment. All reasonable benefits and costs are bundled into the calculation. Table 2.1 summarizes sample components of the benefits and costs buckets.

Table 2.1 Comparing Costs and Benefits

Costs	Benefits
Capital expenditures such as hardware and software	Operational savings/reduced spending such as reduced costs of campaigns or customer identification
Professional services such as consultants or analysts	Increased revenue from the new capabilities

Table 2.1 Comparing Costs and Benefits *(Continued)*

Costs	Benefits
Operational expenses such as resource requirements and development costs	Increased profitability such as lower risk and fee avoidance
Annual expenses such as licensing fees and security costs	Increased productivity/integration across the company such as shared leads and the ability to do more campaigns and detect more fraud instances
Training expenses such as courses, instructors, curriculum, and classroom costs	Improved accuracy/quality such as better target customer lists

Other Financial Metrics for Decision-Making

Business managers spend much of their time calculating financial metrics to provide input into the go/no-go decision for projects. The ROI calculation is just one metric. Some of the other common metrics include the following:

- **Cost of capital** is the rate of return that a company would otherwise earn (at the same risk level) as the investment being analyzed. This calculation depends on the use of the funds, not the source of the funds. Cost of capital is expressed as a percentage (%).

- **Net present value (NPV)** is the value, in today's currency, of a stream of cash inflows and outflows. The NPV takes into account both the cash outflows and inflows to create a net value for the investment. To calculate NPV, you factor in an inflation rate, which makes cash in the future worth a bit less than cash today. NPV is expressed in currency ($).

- **Internal rate of return (IRR)** is the percentage of income in a discounted cash flow analysis of the investment. This calculation takes into account the cash outflows and inflows and creates the percentage return. Decisions often examine the IRR to make sure it is more than a hurdle rate—a minimum-acceptable rate of return for the company. IRR is expressed as a percentage (%)

- **Payback** is the amount of time it takes for the cash inflows to equal the cash outflows. Payback normally is expressed in terms of time (months or years).

Other Considerations in Analytics ROI

A simple ROI works well when the costs and benefits are known and easily calculated and when the benefits are clearly a result of the investment. In analytics projects, however, the complexity of the actual business environment means that the inputs to the ROI calculation may not be as evident or as trustworthy as necessary to make the decision. Furthermore, it is often difficult to isolate the investment in the analytics project from the actual business opportunity, further complicating the decision to make the investment. Analytics are often used to optimize or improve the returns from another business opportunity—for example, to provide better targeting in the direct-mail example described earlier. Finally, the different functions within the organization have different priorities, which often factor into the ROI discussions.

The complexity of the business environment makes it difficult to identify the investment's actual costs and benefits. Inputs can be loosely defined as the people, the process, and the technology necessary to complete the project. Obvious inputs include the costs of the analytics model and the analyst's/modeler's time. Obvious benefits are the cost savings accrued by targeting the customers who come from the application of the model to the database and the additional revenue or accuracy that results from a more targeted group. But the list of actual items to be included in the bucket of inputs can grow quickly when you consider all the resources that go into the analytics program. Some additional questions to ask might include the following:

- What portion of the costs of the IT infrastructure software and hardware are directly part of this project?
- What will it cost to prepare the data for the project (such as building a data warehouse)? What fraction of those costs should be allocated to the analytics initiative?
- What experts or analysts will be needed for this project? What is the cost of including these experts?

You also might want to ask further questions about the potential benefits of the analytical initiative:

- Could improved analytics increase the potential business value? Would additional throughput, timeliness to market, and so on offer value? Will additional revenue or customer retention result?

- What is the value of the additional efficiencies gained by this project? Is there value to a reduction in the data preparation, model development, or model deployment time? What is the value of the labor cost savings?
- Have the operating costs in the IT infrastructure (such as disk space, network, personnel needed to manage and support the efforts) been reduced?

Evaluation of the analytics investment is easily confused with investment in the business project itself because analytics and models can be integral to the business project. For example, in our hypothetical scenario of the direct-mail campaign, some costs of the targeted campaign (the mailing, the postage, the labor necessary to create the campaign) should not be charged to the analytics used to target the campaign (although the savings relative to an untargeted campaign might be credited to analytics). These costs can be a factor in the go/no-go decision about the direct-mail campaign. However, do not confuse the decision of whether to use the analytics modeling approach with the campaign decision itself. Carefully articulate the costs and benefits of both decisions to avoid this confusion. The question to ask is "How do we get value from an investment in analytics?" and not "What is the value of the analytics?" The first question is about the incremental value of the use of the models. The second question is about the overall business project.

The Teradata Method for Evaluating Analytics Investments

Teradata (an underwriter of IIA) has articulated a well-structured business value assessment process. The steps of this process are as follows:

- Phase 1: Validate business goals and document best-practice usage.
- Phase 2: Envision new capabilities.

- Phase 3: Determine ROI and present findings.
- Phase 4: Communicate.

Let's look at each phase in a bit more detail.

Phase 1: Validate Business Goals and Document Best Practices

This phase helps uncover strategic business initiatives and documents how business leaders measure progress. Business strategies to strengthen market advantage, fix weaknesses, and position the enterprise to take advantage of market opportunities are usually based on having an infrastructure of well-managed data and analytical tools. Understanding what the business wants to achieve and how it's doing compared to those objectives highlights areas where value can be obtained. Documenting best practices involves reviewing annual reports, strategic plans, investor presentations, corporate reports, and other shared communications. It also includes interviewing business executives and management to understand business strategy, organizational metrics, operational processes, business capabilities, and linkages between business objectives and data. The outputs of this phase are a clear picture of the current environment and the vision of the new environment from a data and analysis perspective, as well as how they impact business results.

The challenge, according to Teradata executives, is validating the financial impact of the improvements. Here are some of the key categories where this impact appears:

- Increased revenue
- Increased savings
- Reduced spending
- Increased profitability
- Business impact of increased productivity
- Business impact of improved accuracy
- Business impact of increased quality
- Fee avoidance from less risk
- Increased output
- Reduced cycle time

Participants in this assessment are senior managers from the business, the information systems organization, operational units impacted by this investment, and the finance organization, to help validate the calculations.

Phase 2: Envision New Capabilities

In this phase, new capabilities are envisioned and documented, and their potential value is calculated. Managers are encouraged to think broadly about how this infrastructure might be used beyond the business problems at hand. Here are some areas where this value hides

- The ability to answer critical business questions beyond those on the table today
- New ways to attract and keep profitable customers
- New capabilities to drive profitable customer behavior
- Identification of unprofitable activities
- Additional business processes that can be improved

Creating this vision and quantifying the benefits is often the critical step in justifying a borderline infrastructure investment. It shows additional value to the organization beyond the problems and opportunities at hand today.

Phase 3: Determine ROI and Present Findings

Creating the business case is the key activity of this next phase. For each of the business opportunities identified in Phases 1 and 2, a business case is made, articulating the financial impact and business value. The summary of all these cases, coupled with the costs of providing the service (the people, technology, and operating costs) over the term of the anticipated value, provides the data for calculating the investment's ROI and NPV.

This business case is then shared with decision-makers and discussed to identify recommendations, concerns, additional ways to leverage the data, further improvements in processes, and implementation methods to further increase business capabilities. Furthermore, this phase of the process creates a plan to regularly assess business value to ensure that value is obtained, documented, and on track.

Phase 4: Communicate

A successful business value process includes a plan to communicate and market the results to the broader organization. The value created from analytics programs can be difficult to imagine. Skeptics abound until they are shown hard examples of the direct value from the investment. Therefore, a well-thought-out communications plan is essential to set a foundation for future value decisions. The goal of this step is to make visible, throughout the company, the value of the analytics investment and, ultimately, to fuel a culture that values data-driven decision-making.

An Example of Calculating the Value[1]

Teradata shared this example to help make this process more concrete. Using the business value assessment process, the client validated the IT cost savings from migrating the technology to a new system and documented business value from performance improvements and business opportunities. The client estimated that it enjoyed a 30% performance improvement, resulting in a validated savings of $10 million in IT costs over five years.

In addition, the client found that deeper analysis of more-detailed data resulted in significant performance improvement, and new opportunities resulted from improved data management. In one case, the client found a pricing opportunity that recovered $37 million of direct margin and, in another case, an additional $12 million from increased productivity. The client was able to analyze three times as many complex business issues per year as it did prior to the investment. Strategic initiatives that required the analysis of integrated data were identified that enabled the client to compete more effectively. Processes were streamlined, missing data elements were uncovered, and management work was offloaded, all enabling the company to drive revenue and profitability through new initiatives.

Know Your Audience and Proceed Carefully

In our experience, the ROI analysis typically has three audiences: the finance group, the IT group, and the business group in which the analytical investment will take place. Each has a different perspective and seeks a different angle on the issue of return on investment:

- **The finance group** prefers hard numbers in the calculation of cost and benefits. It takes a disciplined look at NPV, IRR, and ROI as part of a portfolio approach to investment management. It seeks to answer the question "How does this investment compare to the other investments in our portfolio?"

- **The IT group** tends to see a more detailed calculation of operating costs—things such as floor space, people, additional servers and disk space, support costs, and software licenses. It seeks to answer the question "What are the additional costs to our data infrastructure?"

- **The business group** is most interested in the project's business value. It seeks to answer the questions "What is the return on my investment?" and "What is the business value?"

When calculating the ROI of an analytics investment, the analyst must be prepared for all three angles. The complete picture is necessary to ensure that all functions are appropriately supportive of the investment and the project. In the following example at Freescale Semiconductor, each of these groups was involved in the financial assessment of analytics investments. But in this case the finance organization was more a user of analytics than an evaluator of investments.

Analytics ROI at Freescale Semiconductor

When Sam Coursen took the reins of the IT organization at Freescale Semiconductor[2] (www.freescale.com), he found an enterprise-wide data initiative under way, but at a very early stage. Having worked on a similar initiative in his previous role as chief information officer (CIO) at NCR Corporation, Coursen was able to apply lessons learned to help guide the transformation at Freescale. One of his initial top-three initiatives at Freescale was an "enterprise-wide data and analytics platform to enable faster and more informed business decision making," according to an interview he gave to *InformationWeek*'s Global CIO columnist in April 2008.[3] By December 2010, Coursen's plans were well on their way to repeating the success he experienced at NCR.

Background and Context

Coursen is vice president and CIO of Freescale Semiconductor. Prior to Freescale, he was vice president and CIO at NCR, which owned Teradata at the time. While at NCR, Coursen led a seven-year journey to create a completely integrated enterprise-wide data warehouse to increase operational efficiency and facilitate better decision-making at all levels of the company. At Freescale, he created similar processes using the lessons he learned at NCR. He is on target to complete a similar transformation in a short five years.

Beginning with High-Impact Areas

The journey at Freescale began with the identification of two areas where business analytics could have a big impact. Coursen sought out places in the organization where colleagues were already interested in getting value from their data. He also sought out projects where the value was quantifiable, in part so that he could show hard value, rather than soft value, to his colleagues.

He found willing partners in finance and manufacturing. In finance, all the sales orders were recorded in one place. Although rich with data, the team was missing efficiency in analyzing and using that data. Manufacturing was ripe for analytics since analyzing end-to-end processes required one-off projects to collect information from all the plants. It could take two weeks to answer seemingly simple questions such as "What trends should we be managing across our plants?" and "We know we have a problem in our Asia plant. Do we have a similar problem in our Phoenix plant?" Similar questions that required data across processes or locations were equally difficult to answer.

Starting with these two applications, Coursen's team identified the key objectives for investing in analytics. For manufacturing, because yields directly affected bottom-line revenue, there was a good measure of the effectiveness of the investment in analytics. The benefits in finance were harder to quantify. The time to close the books (man-hours) and similar metrics became the measures for identifying value. According to Coursen, "Some are hard benefits; others are soft. I don't try to put a dollar amount on the soft benefits. Senior managers understand that. They appreciate that some projects have a hard ROI while others are more subjective, based on management's judgment. Ultimately success translates into value, but making it more explicit isn't really reasonable, and it can undermine efforts that will truly add value. I don't do that."

Getting Managers and Leaders Onboard

Next, Coursen's team created a governance team. Senior-level managers from all divisions were rallied to form this team. Each group contributed at least one part-time member. The team assisted with tool selection, implementation, and promotion within their respective functional areas.

At Freescale, finance was one of the first business functions to pilot an analytics initiative. The project's objective was to source financial data and provide value-added finance solutions. Initial areas of focus were revenue, orders, profit and loss, and operating expenses. Because the information most chief financial officers (CFOs) require was housed in different systems across most companies, little integration occurred end-to-end. In internal meetings, everyone used different numbers to build the same metrics. The first phase was to get all the data into a data warehouse so that, as the reports were circulated, everyone would see the same numbers. Phase 2 was more about predictive analytics and looking to the future. "We now have a clear picture instantaneously about what just happened end-to-end and across entities," Coursen said. "We didn't have that visibility before. Some of our finance colleagues think it's magic."

In manufacturing, early initiatives included a factory data consolidation project and a corporate yield dashboard. These initiatives were chosen because the data was available locally, but not centrally, across factories and because it was directly related to the bottom line, so ROI was relatively easy to calculate. According to Coursen, "We wanted to know how to increase yield from a batch of silicon chips we produced. But we couldn't see end-to-end, so we couldn't improve the process as effectively."

The manufacturing organization audited actual savings and the incidents of savings on an ongoing basis. They recorded the real value they found on a monthly basis, rather than having the analytics group document savings. They found that it saved engineers a significant amount of time and gave capacity for things that couldn't be done in the past.

Manufacturing told this story, not IT or the analytics group, and that added credibility to the investment. In fact, Freescale won several awards for this initiative. One was the Progressive Manufacturer of the Year High Achiever Award for 2010 from *Managing Automation*, an industry magazine. Freescale won this award for its Advanced Intelligent Manufacturing (AIM) project, which used advanced IT to significantly improve manufacturing efficiency. A key piece of the AIM project was its analytics capabilities. According to *Managing Automation*, the investment at the time was $39.9 million, and the ROI was reported to be $103 million. Since its implementation, the return has been much higher.

Coursen commented on his strategy of piloting to build momentum: "I could tell after a couple of years that my colleagues were onboard. No one wanted the analytics engine to go down. Everyone wanted to be next in line for development of a new application. We never talked about how long the journey was. We just moved along incrementally. We started with something doable and valuable. Then we leveraged that success into other areas."

Incremental Growth

At Freescale, the enterprise business intelligence capability grew incrementally. Figure 2.1 shows the rate of growth in various activities. It progresses from the start of the rehosting of the data, to a data warehouse, to the implementation of a procurement application in the fourth quarter of 2008.

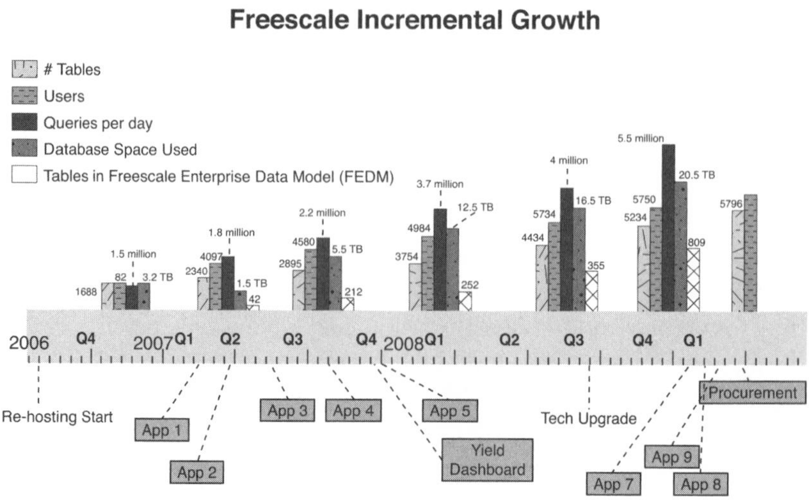

Freescale Incremental Growth

Figure 2.1 Freescale incremental growth.

Lessons Learned

As finance and manufacturing saw success from the analytics projects, word spread quickly across the enterprise, and soon the analytics group was being asked to create applications for other organizations. Here are some of the lessons learned from this experience:

- **The sequencing of initial projects is important.** Start with the high ROI project, not with the low or hard-to-quantify one. The first project normally bears the biggest cost because the start-up usually involves setting up the data warehouse. If it can be done with a large ROI project, future projects are much easier to justify because they have to cover only the incremental costs, such as additional data files.

- **Pick an initial project that has a big pull, where information is scattered all over and a compelling, hard ROI can be calculated.** For example, procurement is a good candidate. Global purchasing is impossible without a clear picture of what is being bought all over the world. When that picture is clear, better prices can be obtained from global suppliers. Applying analytics in the sales function can be soft. Everyone will agree that knowing the customer better is an important objective, but quantifying it is very difficult. Improvements in the supply chain, procurement, and service delivery are more easily quantifiable than better customer satisfaction and better decision-making. Cost is quantifiable, but benefits are not always quantifiable.

- **Componentize the analytics investment as much as possible.** At Freescale, Coursen didn't want to ask for the investment necessary to do the entire enterprise model at the beginning. Instead, he started with a request for funding for the first piece—the pilots for the finance and manufacturing functions. Then, as the requests snowballed, he was able to justify additional investments with the projects that would use the analytics assets.

- **Get good first-use cases, and share them widely to build momentum.** At Freescale, Coursen started with finance and manufacturing, in part because their leaders were willing participants and in part because they had low-hanging fruit that could produce well-accepted ROI. At NCR, Coursen used a similar strategy, starting with services, which directly benefited customers and therefore was a high-visibility application. An early application of analytics capabilities increased the quality of services; it would save some money and increase revenue. It was a conservative estimate and therefore believable, and it turned into an excellent use case that quickly spread across the company.

- **Don't expect an enterprise-wide business analytics program to happen overnight; it takes time.** At NCR, the enterprise business intelligence program took seven years to become a well-accepted part of the business. At Freescale, it's taking about five years.

- **The leadership team sets the tone, but heavy client involvement makes it a success.** IT should not go off in a corner and develop the solution. Every project needs a champion in the function. The leadership team at Freescale insisted on process improvements, standardization, and simplification, in addition to automation and system changes, making this a broader program than just analytics. But requirements definitions, design reviews, testing, and postmortems were done with heavy business-partner involvement, which increased value and quickened adoption.

Endnotes

1. The source of this example is the Teradata whitepaper titled "The Teradata Approach to Assessing the Business Value of Data Warehousing and Analytics Investments," by Corinna Gilbert, Teradata Corporation, 2008. Used here with permission of Teradata.

2. More details on the Freescale example are available at these websites: www.cio.com/article/print/152450 http://shashwatdc.blogspot.com/2007/07/sam-coursens-interview.html www.freescale.com/webapp/sps/site/homepage.jsp?code=COMPANY_INFO_HOME&tid=FSH.

3. Source: www.informationweek.com/news/global-cio/interviews/showArticle.jhtml?articleID=207400183.

Part II
Application of Analytics

3

Leveraging Proprietary Data for Analytical Advantage

Thomas H. Davenport

It is widely agreed that proprietary information provides competitive advantage, but it is scarcely useful without analysis and application in business processes. Data that no other organization possesses can provide insights and allow decisions and actions of which no other organization is capable. Data by itself normally confers little or no direct advantage, but analytics based on data can be very powerful competitive tools. At a time where traditional bases of competitive differentiation have largely faded away, leveraging unique and proprietary data can be a powerful source of competitive differentiation.

Proprietary data can provide a powerful view into company operations and the preferences and behaviors of customers and markets. In many cases, such data is valuable to other companies, competitors, consumers, and even governments. Internet leaders such as Google and Yahoo! have used proprietary data to spur new businesses and offer opportunities for discovery and growth, demonstrating that the data has value beyond first-line marketing opportunities.

Proprietary data is often a by-product of pursuing another business goal, such as executing payment transactions in banking, managing inventory in retail, fulfilling shipments, operating a communication network, or improving Internet searches. Few companies have invested the time and resources necessary to leverage such proprietary data for other uses. But those that have done so have been able to launch new products, provide outstanding customer service, and outperform their competitors. For example, Capital One mines customer data for new-product development, Progressive insurance uses proprietary data on customer driving behavior in its Snapshot program to accurately price car insurance, and Delta Dental of California analyzes claims data to identify cost savings. In many cases, the discoveries in the data led to new business opportunities that were otherwise not obvious.

Proprietary data is also being used for advantage in sports. Daryl Morey, general manager of the NBA Houston Rockets, is one of the most analytical managers in professional basketball. He argues that "real advantage comes from unique data," and he employs a number of analysts who classify the defensive moves of opposing players in every NBA game. The Boston Red Sox follow the same philosophy. They have traveled to NCAA headquarters to categorize and quantify the paper-based records of college baseball players to analyze what attributes lead to success in the professional leagues. The Italian professional soccer team AC Milan gathers proprietary data on its players' movement patterns under different conditions and uses it to predict and prevent injuries.

Recently, new businesses have developed around the goal of creating and mining new types of data for business gain through using social networks, selling data-derived products, or participating as marketplace creators. Many of these organizations refer to themselves as big-data firms. One company, Factual, is attempting to gather a large mass of proprietary data on a variety of seemingly unrelated topics. One account of the company described its data-gathering strategy:

> Geared to both big companies and smaller software developers, it includes available government data, terabytes of corporate data and information on 60 million places in 50 countries, each described by 17 to 40 attributes. Factual knows more than 800,000 restaurants in 30 different ways, including location, ownership and ratings by diners and health boards. It also contains information on half a billion Web pages, a list of America's high schools and data on the offices, specialties and insurance preferences of 1.8 million United States health care professionals. There are also listings of 14,000 wine grape varietals, of military aircraft accidents from 1950 to 1974, and of body masses of major celebrities.[1]

However, the role of such data and its potential for spurring innovation, new sources of revenue, and new business and operational risks is still largely unexplored.

A 2009 Accenture survey of 600 executives in the U.S. and U.K. suggests that proprietary data is rare but extremely valuable. Only 10% of the survey respondents said that their company's proprietary data "far exceeds that of the competition in terms of usefulness or significance, offering us a distinct competitive advantage." Similarly, 86% said their company data was "about on par with that of the competition." Yet when asked how valuable proprietary data can be in differentiating a company and its products from the competition, 97% said it was either "very valuable" or "quite valuable."

Why such high levels of perceived value and low levels of activity with regard to proprietary data? It might be argued that most organizations and managers lack familiarity with the topic and haven't really embedded it within discussions on strategy and competition.

Issues with Managing Proprietary Data and Analytics

Despite the fact that most managers acknowledge the value of proprietary data and analytics based on them, there are still more questions than answers about the topic. Here are some of the specific questions that organizations should address before actively pursuing proprietary data strategies:

- What are the best sources of proprietary data for my business?
- How should we convert proprietary data into proprietary insights through analytics? How do the opportunities vary by business line and strategy?
- What types of proprietary data have the most potential for competitive differentiation? How are competitors likely to respond?
- Do proprietary data and analytics have the potential in our industry to disrupt and reshape industry dynamics?
- Should we sell our proprietary data or analytics, or keep them to ourselves?

- When should we consider working with an intermediary data provider to market such data or analytics?
- In addition to selling our data, what other means of achieving value from proprietary data and analytics exist?
- How can we leverage data and analysis from third parties and syndicated sources for competitive advantage?

To address and answer these questions systematically and regularly, companies need to develop institutionalized approaches. Some organizations do so via executive-level data steering committees. Others have created Chief Data Officer positions, particularly in financial services. In any case, data-oriented discussions should address not only the problems that organizations encounter in data management, but also the opportunities arising from proprietary data and analytics.

In addition to the strategic opportunities from proprietary data and analytics, there are also organizational and regulatory implications to be explored. Because such data may contain enormous amounts of sensitive customer information, the role of a privacy protocol (especially in the presence of little regulation) is a real concern. Customer expectations brought forth by technology—such as on-demand services, remote banking, frequent-shopper identification, and transportable electronic medical records—further raise important issues. These issues include how a company should manage its data and the circumstances under which data can and should be shared across companies.

To illustrate some of the opportunities and challenges inherent in proprietary data, I'll describe two cases. One involves a proprietary data initiative in an organization; the other addresses the potential for proprietary data in an entire industry—and the somewhat puzzling failure to achieve it.

Leveraging Proprietary Data in One Organization: PaxIS from IATA

To briefly illustrate some of the potential competitive advantages and perils in using proprietary data, consider the case of PaxIS, which stands for Passenger Intelligence Services, from the International Air

Transport Authority (IATA). PaxIS employed proprietary data—or at least data that IATA believed was proprietary—on flights across 163 countries captured through the authority's billing and settlement plan (BSP). By many accounts, international airlines found the data useful for such purposes as market share analyses, network planning and optimization, fleet planning, pricing and revenue management, marketing planning, and analysis of sales by travel agency channel. IATA sold access to PaxIS but largely relied on its airline customers to analyze the data. The authority also sold information on airline schedules (known as the Schedule Reference Service [SRS]) as a useful companion to the PaxIS passenger demand information.

However, some providers of computerized airline reservations systems (collectively known as global distribution systems [GDSs]) argued that IATA did not actually own the data, given it was collected and transmitted through reservation systems. One GDS, Amadeus, took legal action against the PaxIS offering, arguing that PaxIS constituted a breach of contract by IATA. Amadeus also charged that because new European Commission regulations prohibited it from identifying specific travel agency sales, IATA should not be allowed to do so either. In 2009, an International Chamber of Commerce arbitration panel found in favor of Amadeus and prohibited IATA from using its data in PaxIS. In 2011, the European Commission ruled that PaxIS had to remove all European data from the system. Throughout this period, Amadeus began to market its own proprietary data offering called Amadeus Market Information (previously known as Marketing Information Data Tapes [MIDT]). This offering also compiled data from travel agency flight bookings and could be used for purposes similar to PaxIS.

The case of PaxIS illustrates both the potential and the peril of leveraging proprietary data. Such data can be valuable to many participants in a value chain and can yield additional revenue and profits. But it may be subject to regulation, ownership disputes, competition, and difficulties of aggregation and management. In addition, to be of use either internally or to customers, proprietary data must be analyzed and used in business processes involving decisions and actions.

Leveraging Proprietary Data in an Industry: Consumer Payments

Every day, billions of consumer payments—credit and debit card transactions, checks, money transfers, and online payments—pass through the financial system. Several types of organizations may have access to payment data, including banks, credit card networks (Visa and MasterCard), financial transaction processors (FiServ and First Data), and financial planning and management software firms and websites (Intuit, Wesabe.com). What these institutions have in common is that they don't take much advantage of the payments data they possess. As one executive at a firm with payments data put it, "We studied the opportunity to exploit payments data. To the team it looked like bags of money just sitting on a table. But my company just didn't want to do anything with it." There are many reasons for this reluctance to seize the opportunity that payments data represents, which I describe next.

There are at least three major ways to utilize payments data for positive business advantage. A couple of additional ways, fraud prevention and credit risk analysis, are intended more to prevent business disadvantage and therefore are not covered in detail in this chapter. However, many financial institutions regularly examine payments data for evidence of fraud and cancel a transaction in real time if they suspect a fraudulent payment. Some banks and credit card providers have correlated certain types of payments with higher levels of credit risk. Each of the three more-positive approaches is described next, along with the possible reasons why owners of payment data may not have exploited the opportunity.

Macroeconomic Intelligence and Capital Markets

Organizations with large amounts of payments data can use it to analyze and act on the state of the economy in particular countries or regions. A bank with substantial scale in credit cards, for example, has data on what customers are spending on what products. In many cases it can compile and analyze data faster than government sources. Using this data, the bank (or agents or customers it sells the analysis to) could invest in firms, industries, or financial instruments that benefit from the spending patterns. This is not a hypothetical example; both CitiGroup and Bank of America have used consumer spending data from credit cards to place such bets. All accounts suggest that they tend to be successful. As one banker put it, "We can predict the GDP a couple of weeks before the Fed announces it, and as a result we've made lots of money in the hedge markets." Even this bullish executive, however, admitted that his bank was only scratching the surface of what could be done with payments data in this regard.

What prevents other banks and payments processors from making macroeconomic bets? Many firms that would have such data don't have in-house capital markets groups that could make the necessary investments. Of course, they could invest through other firms, but this seems less likely to happen in practice. Making investments on macroeconomic data also may not fit with some firms' business models. Another constraint may be the lack of economic and analytical skills in organizations to do the analysis and make investment decisions. Some banks have also been cautious in this area because they fear objections by regulatory bodies.

Targeted Marketing

Payment data provides a wealth of opportunities for learning about customers and targeting offers to them. Through it an organization can learn about discretionary and nondiscretionary spending, loyalty, life events, price elasticity behavior, and payment behavior. This makes it an ideal tool for targeted marketing to the most desirable consumers for products and services.

Actual uses of payment data for targeted marketing thus far, however, have been somewhat limited. A few banks have explored the potential of payments data to identify cross-selling opportunities. For example, if a bank detects through analyzing check payments that a customer is making payments on credit cards from other banks, the bank can offer the customer a preferred rate on its own credit card. Citizens Bank has employed targeting for online offers based on payment behaviors; the offers are for its own products and those of marketing partners and affiliates.

In addition to targeted offers, payments data can be used to segment customers for differential pricing. Pricing can be based on the usage volume, profitability, or lifetime value of services used. Some credit card firms, such as Capital One, have used this approach to charge different prices for "transactors" (those who pay off their bills in full each month) versus "revolvers," who use their credit cards to take loans by not paying bills in full.

Payment data analysis also has value in predicting which customers are most likely to leave. A study of payment data by eCom Advisors for one bank found that the customers most likely to leave the bank did not make electronic bill payments or did so rarely and were relatively young. Targeted marketing to specific consumer profiles (young and low activity) can decrease attrition and maximize profitability.

Banks, the most likely users of payments data for targeted marketing, have been reluctant to apply it for this purpose. Many bankers focus primarily on brand-oriented marketing, rather than on targeted direct marketing. In addition, they may be nervous about negative customer reactions to targeted marketing based on payment data analysis. Some firms in other domains (Google, Groupon) have been very successful with targeted marketing based on analyzing consumer data. However, still other firms (Coca-Cola, Facebook, Amazon) have encountered resistance to targeted marketing initiatives based on customer behavior data analysis. In 2012, Bank of America began offering targeted offers (primarily of nonbanking products and services) based on payments data to debit card customers. The bank employed a third party, Cardlytics, to analyze the data.

Enhanced Customer Services

A final alternative in taking advantage of payment data is to provide information-based customer service offerings for personal financial management. A variety of potential services can be provided. Thus far, most of the providers of such services have been online startups (Mint.com, acquired by Intuit; Wesabe; Geezeo) and PC software (Quicken, Microsoft Money) that offer account aggregation, budgeting and investing tools, and financial education. Several of the sites also offer "Web 2.0" services, in which users can discuss their financial situations with others. A few also offer recommendations on products and services that the user already uses, such as a cellular telephone provider with lower rates than the one the user currently uses. Banks (such as Wells Fargo's "My Spending Report") and credit card firms offer a somewhat lower level of services involving spending reports and categorizations.

Third-party firms, of course, don't have direct access to payments data and must get access to customer accounts by obtaining customer permission and linkages to their financial providers. Payment processors also typically don't have relationships with consumers. Again, banks are the most likely to benefit from enhanced services to customers based on payment data analysis, but they have been curiously slow in pursuing these options.

Data Ownership and Permissions Issues in Payments

Consumers own their financial transaction data and generally must "opt in" to any plan to use data for marketing or enhanced services. Of course, most do so automatically when they open their accounts. There is good reason for the conservative approaches banks have displayed toward payments data. Consumers usually consider their spending habits to be personal and inviolate and probably would react negatively to unsophisticated marketing approaches that don't provide them with clear benefits. This doesn't mean, however, that well-planned efforts to employ payment data analysis won't succeed. There is much opportunity to exploit this resource, but it should be handled carefully and with great attention to the privacy and security of customer data.

Lessons Learned from Payments Data

Many potential benefits are possible from leveraging and analyzing proprietary data, but most opportunities have not been aggressively pursued. It is always difficult to understand why something hasn't happened, but the reasons organizations have not aggressively pursued this opportunity range from inertia, to lack of understanding of the possibilities, to regulatory uncertainty. To take advantage of the opportunities provided by proprietary data, companies may need an appropriate organizational structure (or partnerships with other firms); this could be another reason why many firms have hesitated. Data ownership and permission for use are other key factors to address in exploiting proprietary data.

Judging from actions by financial services firms thus far, there may be fewer concerns around preventing negative actions (such as fraud and credit default risk) than creating positive benefits (such as targeted marketing and customized offers).

Endnote

1. Quentin Hardy, "Just the Facts. Yes, All of Them," *New York Times*, March 24, 2012. Page 1, Sunday Business section.

4

Analytics on Web Data:
The Original Big Data

Bill Franks

Wouldn't it be great to understand customer intent instead of just customer action? Wouldn't it be great to understand your customers' thought processes as they decide whether they'll make a purchase? In the past it was virtually impossible to get answers to such questions. Today, they can be answered with the use of detailed web data. That's what this chapter is all about.

There is no better way to understand what big data is all about than to see some specific examples of big data and how it can be used. Perhaps no big-data source is as widely used today as web data.

Note

The content for this chapter is based on a conference talk created with my colleague Rebecca Bucnis. We also generated a white paper on the topic "Taking Your Analytics Up a Notch by Integrating Clickstream Data" for SAS Global Forum 2011.

The content for this chapter was also published in *Taming the Big Data Tidal Wave: Finding Opportunities in Huge Data Streams with Advanced Analytics.* © 2012 Bill Franks. (John Wiley & Sons, Inc. Used with permission of John Wiley & Sons, Inc.)

Organizations across a number of industries have integrated detailed, customer-level behavioral data sourced from websites into their enterprise analytics environments. Most organizations, however, still end web integration with the inclusion of online transactions.

Traditional web analytics vendors provide operational reporting on click-through rates, traffic sources, and metrics based only on web data. However, detailed web behavior data historically was not leveraged outside of web reporting.

Leading companies have shown that detailed web data can provide previously untapped corporate value. This chapter outlines what those leaders are doing, why they are doing it, and why every organization should consider such analytics today. The examples are compelling and promise to be eye-opening to those who have never given much thought to integrating detailed clickstream data with other data as opposed to keeping it isolated.

The core theme of this chapter isn't simply the taming of web data. Instead of aggregated web metrics from a distinct data silo, organizations should focus on integrating web data with all the other relevant information about their customers. Utilizing such information in a scalable analytics environment lets you move beyond purchasing insights about customers and into individual intentions, purchase decision processes, and preferences. Tapping into the rich insight provided by this new data source, an organization can make huge strides forward.

How does an organization capture, analyze, and utilize this rich information to drive insight? First, we'll discuss what data needs to be acquired and why. Then we'll explore some examples of what that data can reveal. Finally, we'll discuss specific examples of how analytics processes can be transformed through the integration of web data. Web data is one big-data source that many organizations have already tamed. Add yours to the list!

Web Data Overview

Organizations have talked about having a 360-degree view of their customers for years. At any point in time, one organization or another claims that it has achieved a true 360-degree view. In reality, it is impossible to have a true 360-degree view because this implies that you know everything there is to know about your customers. When a 360-degree view is discussed, what is really meant is that the organization has as full a view of its customers as possible considering the technology and data available at that point in time. However, the finish line is always moving. Just when you think you have finally arrived, the finish line moves farther out again.

A few decades ago, companies were at the top of their game if they had the names and addresses of their customers and could append demographic information to those names through the then-new third-party data enhancement services. Eventually, cutting-edge companies started to attach basic recency, frequency, and monetary (RFM) value metrics to customers. Such metrics look at when a customer last purchased (recency), how often she has purchased (frequency), and how much she spent (monetary value). These RFM summaries might be tallied for the past year and possibly over the customer's lifetime. In the past 10 to 15 years, virtually all businesses have started to collect and analyze their customers' detailed transaction histories. This had led to an explosion of analytical power and a much deeper understanding of customer behavior.

Update Your 360-Degree View

Many organizations haven't yet moved beyond yesterday's standard transactional view of customers. The integration of new data sources, such as web data, is now possible and is driving huge value for early adopters. Is your organization's view of its customers up to date?

Many organizations are frozen at the transactional history stage. Although this stage is still important, many companies incorrectly assume that this is still the closest they will get to a 360-degree view of their customers. Today, organizations need to collect newly evolving big-data sources related to their customers from a variety of extended and newly emerging touchpoints such as web browsers, mobile applications, kiosks, social media sites, and more.

Just as transactional data enabled a revolution in the power and depth of analysis, so too do these new data sources let you take analytics to a new level. With today's data storage and processing capabilities, it is absolutely possible to achieve success, and many forward-thinking companies have already proven it by applying the data to a variety of problems, some of which we'll discuss shortly.

What Are You Missing?

Have you ever stopped to think about what happens if only the transactions generated by a website are captured? Perhaps for a website, 95% of browsing sessions do not result in the creation of a shopping basket. Of the 5% that do, only about half, or 2.5%, actually begin the checkout process. And of that 2.5%, only two-thirds, or 1.7%, actually complete a purchase. These figures are not unrealistic in many cases.

What this means is that information is missing on more than 98% of web sessions if only transactions are tracked. But more important, an even higher percentage of available data is missing. For every purchase transaction, dozens or hundreds of specific actions might be taken on the site to get to that sale. That information needs to be collected and analyzed alongside the final sales data.

It is important to note that this is not just the same old web analytics story from years past. Traditional web analytics focus on aggregated behavior, summarized in an environment where only web data was included. The goal needs to be moving beyond reporting summary statistics, even if they can be viewed in some detail, to actually combining customer-level web behavior data with other cross-channel customer data. This is moving far beyond clickthrough reports and page view summaries.

Just as RFM is only a small piece of what transaction data can yield, so too are traditional web analytics only a portion of what web data can yield. Web data is a game-changing, amazing new frontier that can revolutionize organizations' customer insights and the impacts those insights have on their businesses.

Imagine the Possibilities

Imagine knowing everything customers do as they go through the process of doing business with your organization. Not just what they buy, but what they are thinking about buying, along with the key decision criteria they use. Such knowledge enables a new level of understanding about your customers and a new level of interaction. It allows you to meet their needs more quickly and keep them satisfied.

- Imagine you are a retailer. Imagine walking through the aisles with customers and recording every place they go, every item they look at, every item they pick up, every item they put in the cart and then take back out. Imagine knowing whether they read nutritional information, if they look at laundry instructions, if they read the promotional brochure on the shelf, or if they look at other information made available to them in the store.

- Imagine you are a bank. Imagine being able to identify every credit card option customers consider. Imagine being able to understand if it was a reward program, interest rates, or annual fees that drove their choice. Imagine knowing what they say about each product after they own it.

- Imagine you are an airline. Imagine being able to identify every flight customers view before choosing their final itinerary. Imagine knowing if they care more about price or convenience. Imagine knowing all the destinations they consider and when they first consider them.

- Imagine you are a telecom company. Imagine being able to identify every phone model, rate plan, data plan, and accessory customers consider before making a final decision. Imagine knowing that they came back to your site by typing into a search engine "renew contract" or "contract cancellation."

It certainly sounds exciting to have the information outlined in this list. You can have it right now by making a commitment to collect it and make it available for analytics. Organizations in each of these industries are already doing so.

A Fundamentally New Source of Information

The beauty of exploring customers' detailed web behavior is that it moves beyond just knowing what they buy. You can now gain insights into how they make their decisions. Instead of seeing just the result, you have visibility into the entire buying process. This big-data source isn't a simple extension of existing data sources. Many organizations were excited about the integration of web transactions with traditional transactions. But, at its core, a web transaction is simply another transaction record with a new "transaction type" or "transaction location" flag. In the case of detailed web behavior, there is no existing analog for most of the data that can be collected. It is a fundamentally new source of information.

A Rare Opportunity

It isn't often that an organization has the opportunity to collect a completely new and distinct set of data. Detailed web data is one of the rare opportunities to do so. There simply isn't an existing data source that provides much of what web data provides outside of expensive surveys or research studies that provide data on only a small subset of customers.

One of the most exciting aspects of web data is that it provides factual information on customer preferences, future intentions, and motivations that are virtually impossible to get from other sources outside of a direct conversation or survey. Why do customers choose one offering over another? Perhaps organizations think they know. However, they will likely find that many customers make choices in ways that were not anticipated.

As soon as you know customers' intentions, preferences, and motivations, you have completely new ways of communicating with them, driving further business, and increasing their loyalty. The glorious part of this story happens when you marry web data with everything you have learned from the prior 360-degree view. Now you can extend that view with all the rich new web behavior data available.

What Data Should Be Collected?

If possible, you should capture any action that a customer takes while interacting with an organization. That means detailed event history from any customer touchpoint. Common touchpoints today include websites, kiosks, mobile apps, and social media. You can capture a wide range of customer events:

- Purchases
- Product views
- Shopping basket additions
- Watching a video
- Accessing a download
- Reading/writing a review

- Requesting help
- Forwarding a link
- Posting a comment
- Registering for a webinar
- Executing a search

This chapter focuses on web data, but the same principles apply for the other sources listed. The examples that follow are website-centric, but keep in mind that the same concepts apply across the board to all touchpoints from which data can be collected.

It Isn't Just About Web Data

The concepts discussed in this chapter apply to a variety of touch-points. These include things such as kiosks and mobile applications. Don't limit your thinking to web data.

What About Privacy?

Privacy is a big issue today and may become an even bigger issue as time passes. You must seriously consider what data is captured and how it is used. You need to respect not just formal legal restrictions, but also what your customers will view as appropriate. The last thing an organization wants to do is create programs that customers view as being "creepy" or intrusive. Privacy is an issue worthy of a deep discussion within your organization. It is outside the scope of this chapter to cover all the issues surrounding privacy. However, we will examine one option to address privacy concerns while still gaining value from analyzing web data.

Even if an organization wants to be conservative in its actions, there are options for realizing tremendous value from web data. Even if you have no desire to interact with customers individually or tie the data back to identifiable customer data, web data is still valuable. An arbitrary identification number that is not personally identifiable can be matched to each unique customer based on a logon, a cookie, or a similar piece of information. This creates what might be called a "faceless" customer record. Even though all the data associated with one of these identifiers is from one person, the people doing the analysis have no ability to tie the ID back to the actual customer. Analysis can still be done to look for patterns across customers, however. These patterns are powerful and can be found without ever worrying about which specific individual did what.

Consider Faceless Customer Analysis

Much of the value in customer analysis is in the aggregate patterns that can be identified. You only need to identify an individual by name or address if you want to do direct marketing. You can do a lot of high-value analysis simply by looking at faceless customer data. With this approach, analysts only know each customer by an arbitrary, nontraceable number. Don't miss out on the benefits of such analysis.

It is the patterns across faceless customers that matter, not the behavior of any specific customer. The individuals in this example are important only as an input to the pattern analysis. Nobody needs to identify who each individual actually is to derive value. With today's database technologies, analysts can perform analysis without being able to identify the individuals involved. This can remove many privacy concerns. Of course, many organizations do in fact identify and target specific customers as a result of such analytics. They have presumably put in place privacy policies, including opt-out options, and are careful to follow them.

What Web Data Reveals

Now that we've covered what web data is, let's dive into it in more detail. There are a number of specific areas where web data can help organizations understand their customers better than is possible without web data. Without taming this source of big data, such insights will be very difficult, if not impossible, to come by. We'll establish some broad categories of the kinds of insights you can gain from web data in this section before moving on to detailed use cases and applications in the final section.

Shopping Behaviors

A good starting point for understanding shopping behavior is identifying how customers come to a site to begin shopping. What search engine do they use? What specific search terms do they enter? Do they use a bookmark they created previously? Analysts can take this information and look for patterns in terms of which search terms, search engines, and referring sites are associated with higher sales rates. Note that analysts can look into higher sales rates not just within a given web session, but also for the same customer over time. This can be combined with a view of sales on the website along with a cross-channel view of the customer's purchase behavior over time. That is where the value resides.

As soon as customers are on a site, start to examine all the products they explore. Identify who simply looked at a product landing page and left, and who drilled down farther. Who viewed extra photos? Who read product reviews? Who looked at detailed product specifications? Who looked at shipping information? Who took advantage of any other information that is available on the site? For example, identify which products were chosen for a "Compare" view. Last, it is easy to identify which products were added to a wish list or basket, as well as if they were later removed.

Read Your Customers' Minds

Web data is unique in that it allows you to gain insights into what customers are thinking about buying next and how their decision processes work. This lets you be proactive and nudge a customer down a purchase path she has yet to complete. Provide the right offer, and she'll almost think you're reading her mind as she makes a purchase.

One interesting ability enabled by web data is identifying product bundles that are of interest to a customer *before* she makes a purchase. Move beyond trying to up-sell a customer with a follow-up offer after a purchase. Instead, examine what she is browsing and make her an offer to buy a complete bundle in the first place.

For example, consider a customer who views computers, backup disks, printers, and monitors. It is likely the customer is considering a complete PC system upgrade. Offer a package right away that contains the specific mix of items the customer has browsed. Do not wait until the customer purchases the computer and then offer generic bundles of accessories. A customized bundle offer before the customer buys is more powerful than a generic one after she has purchased.

Customer Purchase Paths and Preferences

Using web data, analysts can identify how customers arrive at their buying decisions by watching how they navigate a site. It is possible to gain insight into their preferences. Consider an airline, which can tell a number of things about preferences based on the ticket that is booked. For example, how far in advance was the ticket booked? What fare class was booked? Did the trip span a weekend? This is all useful information, but an airline can get even more from web data.

An airline can identify customers who value convenience. Such customers typically start searches with specific times and direct flights only. They deviate from the most convenient direct flight only if there is a huge price difference for a minimal change in convenience. Perhaps a customer can save $700 by flying into New York's JFK airport instead of LaGuardia. He can land at JFK within 30 minutes of the LaGuardia flight, and the extra cab fare is only about $20. In that case, a convenience-oriented customer might decide $700 in savings is worth the extra hassle of JFK. But if the difference is only $200 and the arrival time is two hours later, a convenience-oriented customer will stick with the more convenient option.

Airlines can also identify customers who value price first and foremost and are willing to consider many flight options to get the best price. Such customers will deviate from the cheapest option only if there is a moderate price difference for a huge gain in convenience.

For example, perhaps a customer can leave at 10 a.m. for $220 versus leaving at 6 a.m. for $200. The four extra hours of sleep are worth $20 to a price-oriented customer, so she pays the $20 premium for the later flight.

Based on search patterns, airlines also can tell how tied to deals or specific destinations a given customer is. Does she research all the special deals available and then choose one of those for her trip? Or does she look only at a certain destination and pay what is required to get there? For example, a college student may be open to any number of spring break destinations and will take the one with the best deal. On the other hand, a customer who regularly visits family will only be interested in flying to where her family is.

Simply knowing that a customer regularly browses weekend deals for certain destinations can be a good indicator of what's important to her. Some customers are open to visiting family whenever they see a deal to the right city. If they see a deal, they book it. Once that pattern is identified, an airline can anticipate customers' needs better.

In the preceding examples, historical insight into purchase history is invaluable when married with current browsing and research patterns. Of course, it takes time and effort to change analytical processes to account for such patterns. But as soon as you know which aspects of a site appeal to customers on an individual basis, you can target them with messages that meet their needs much more effectively.

Research Behaviors

Understanding how customers use a site's research content can lead to tremendous insights into how to interact with each customer. You also can figure out how different aspects of the site do or do not add value in driving sales. As you examine the options customers explore on their way to a purchase, you can infer what is important to them.

For example, consider an online store that sells movies. If some customers routinely look at the standard, widescreen, extended, and HD versions of a movie before making a final decision, that says they are open to various format options even if they often end up buying a certain format most of the time. As soon as you know a customer's patterns, you can alter what she sees when she visits a site to make it easier for her to find her favorite options quickly. A customer who views a lot of formats might be shown all the formats every time. However, why make a customer sort through all DVD formats if you know that she neither browses nor buys anything but a single format?

Another way to use web data to understand customers' research patterns is to identify which pieces of information offered on a site are valued by the customer base overall and by the best customers specifically. How often do customers look at previews, additional photos, or technical specs before making a purchase? Note that when you track across sessions and combine with other customer data, you can know if people researched one day and then bought another day. A final purchase event often is a highly targeted web session that simply executes the purchase. The historical browsing history is needed to put together the whole picture. Perhaps a little-used website feature the organization was considering removing is a big favorite among a critical segment of customers. In that case, the feature might be kept.

The Power of Research

It is no longer necessary to execute expensive, small-scale surveys to gain insights into how customers research and study products before making a purchase. Web data can provide detailed insights into what is important to each customer individually, as well as to customers in aggregate. Plus, it eliminates the risk of having a customer tell you on a survey he'll do one thing when in reality he will do another. You'll see the truth.

An organization might see an unusual number of customers drop a specific product after looking at the detailed specifications page, but not when they don't view the specs. After looking into what is on the page, the company might find that the product description is unclear or that one of the specs is inaccurate. With an updated description, sales increase.

The reading of reviews is a tremendous indicator of what is important to people. Which customers value reviews? Which do not? Which products routinely lose customers after their reviews are read? Reviews have the power to make or break a sale. Once you know which customers usually buy after reading reviews, if you see many of them deciding not to purchase a specific product after reading its reviews, you should look into it. Perhaps some negative reviews are posted. If so, you can identify if they are valid, what points they raise, and how you will address those points.

In the end, identifying which site features are important to each customer and how each customer leverages the site for research can help you better tailor a site to the individual. For customers who always drill down to detailed product specifications, perhaps those specs can come up as soon as a product is viewed. For those who always want to see photos, perhaps photos can be featured in full size instead of as thumbnails. The point is to make research easier for your customers so that they will come to you instead of the competition when they are ready to research and buy.

Feedback Behaviors

Some of the best information customers can provide is detailed feedback on products and services. Simply the fact that customers are willing to take the time to offer feedback indicates that they are engaged with a brand. By using text mining to understand the tone, intent, and topic of a customer's feedback, you begin to get a better picture of what is important to that individual.

Do certain customers regularly post reviews of what they buy? If those reviews are often positive and are read by other customers, it might be a good idea to give such customers special incentives to keep the good words coming. Similarly, if you study the questions and comments submitted via online help chats with customers, you can get a feel not just for what customers in general are asking about, but what each specific customer is asking about. If analysis shows that certain features are always important for a specific customer, point the customer in the direction of other items with similar attributes.

Is a customer a fan of your company on Facebook? Does he or she follow you on Twitter? By looking at the comments and questions customers pose through such interfaces, you can learn much about their likes and dislikes. Additionally, when you identify very active customers who often write about your company on social media sites, you may want to cultivate them as an influential brand ambassador. Give such customers the extra attention they deserve given the influence they have over your brand. Note that customers' influence is not always strongly correlated with their individual value. A midsized customer who usually warrants standard treatment can be very vocal. It may be smart to upgrade him beyond what his dollar value implies due to the influence he wields.

Web Data in Action

What an organization knows about its customers is never the complete picture. You must always make assumptions based on the information available. If you have only a partial view, you often can extrapolate the full view accurately enough to get the job done. But it is also possible that the missing information paints a totally different picture than you expected. In the cases where the missing information differs from the assumptions, you can make suboptimal, if not totally wrong, decisions.

Therefore, organizations should strive to collect and analyze as much data as possible. We've discussed a number of different types of web data and some broad uses of them. Now, let's move on to some specific examples of how organizations can apply web data to enhance existing analytics, enable new analytics, and improve their business.

The Next Best Offer

A very common marketing analysis is predicting the next best offer for each customer. Of all the available options, which single offer should next be suggested to a customer to maximize the chances of success? Having web behavior data can totally change the decision of what a customer's next best offer is and make those decisions much more robust.

Let's assume that you work at a bank and that you know the following information about a customer named Mr. Smith:

- He has four accounts: checking, savings, credit card, and a car loan.
- He makes five deposits and 25 withdrawals per month.
- He never visits a branch in person.
- He has a total of $50,000 in assets deposited.
- He owes a total of $15,000 between his credit card and car loan.

What is the best offer you could email Mr. Smith? Based on his profile, it would be reasonable to argue for any number of things such as a lower credit card interest rate or an offer of a certificate of deposit for his sizable cash holdings. One thing that would not be high on most people's list is offering a mortgage because no data says this choice is remotely relevant. However, when you examine Mr. Smith's web behavior, a couple of key facts jump off the page:

- He browsed mortgage rates five times in the past month.
- He viewed information about homeowners' insurance.
- He viewed information about flood insurance.
- He explored home-loan options (fixed-rate versus variable-rate, 15-year versus 30-year) twice in the past month.

It's pretty easy to decide what to discuss next with Mr. Smith now, isn't it?

Get Ahead of the Curve

With web browsing behavior, it is possible to gain insights that totally change the direction that might otherwise have been taken. Decisions can be based on what a customer has been browsing recently, which in many cases are products or product lines that the customer hasn't purchased before. As soon as the web data alerts you to the unseen opportunity, you can take action to pull the customer into the new product line.

It can be difficult for any business to determine if its customer base is still engaged. The web provides direct clues about what interests customers and if they are still engaged. Consider the case of a catalog retailer that also has many store locations. The cataloger collects the following data for each customer, among other things:

- Last products browsed
- Last products reviewed
- Historical purchases
- Marketing campaign and response history

The data is compiled and analyzed to determine which products each customer appears most interested in. Adjustments are made to the content of catalogs sent, as well as the length of the catalogs and the offers within each. The effort leads to major changes in the cataloger's promotional efforts versus its traditional approach, providing the following results:

- A decrease in total mailings
- A reduction in total catalog promotions pages
- A materially significant increase in total revenues

Web data can help completely overhaul activities for the better.

Attrition Modeling

In the telecommunications industry, companies have invested massive amounts of time and effort to create, enhance, and perfect *churn* models. Churn models flag customers who are most at risk of canceling their accounts so that action can be taken proactively to prevent them from doing so. Churn is a major issue for the industry; huge amounts of money are at stake. The models have a major impact on the bottom line.

Managing customer churn has been, and remains, critical to understanding patterns of customer usage and profitability. Imagine how this has been invigorated today with the use of web data put into the right context. Mrs. Smith, as a customer of telecom Provider 101, goes to Google and types "How do I cancel my Provider 101 contract?" She then follows a link to Provider 101's cancelation policies page. Imagine how much stronger, more time-sensitive, and usable this customer data is for a churn model and for taking meaningful action compared to other data.

It is hard to think of an indicator of cancelation that is stronger than knowing that Mrs. Smith researched canceling—aside from her actually taking the final step of making the cancelation request. Perhaps analysts would have seen her usage dropping, or perhaps not. It would take weeks or months to identify such a change in usage. By capturing Mrs. Smith's actions on the Web, Provider 101 can move more quickly to avert losing her as a customer.

Missing early opportunities to identify customers who are exploring cancelation means trying to win them back when their minds are already made up and another carrier may have already won their business. It will be too late in most cases, and the customer will be lost for good.

Response Modeling

Many models are created to help predict the choice a customer will make when presented with a request for action. Models typically try to predict which customers will make a purchase, or accept an offer, or click a link in an email message. For such models, a technique called *logistic regression* is often used. These models usually are called *response models* or *propensity models*. The attrition model we discussed a moment ago is in the same class of model. The main difference is that in an attrition model, the goal is predicting a negative behavior (churn) rather than a positive behavior (purchase or response).

When using a response or propensity model, all customers are scored and ranked according to their likelihood of taking action. Then appropriate segments are created based on those rankings to reach out to the customers. In theory, every customer has a unique score. In practice, because only a small number of variables define most models, many customers end up with identical or nearly identical scores. This is particularly true of customers who do not spend much or frequently. In such cases, many customers can end up in big groups with very similar, very low scores.

Web data can greatly increase differentiation among customers. This is especially true among low-value or infrequent customers, who can have a large uplift in score based on the web data. Let's look at an example where four customers are scored by a response model with a handful of variables. Each customer in the example has the same score due to having the same value for each of the model's variables. The scores are hypothetical, so don't worry about how they were computed. The four customers' profiles are as follows:

- Last purchase was within 90 days
- Six purchases in the past year
- Spent $200 to $300 total
- Homeowner with estimated household income of $100,000 to $150,000
- Member of the loyalty program
- Has purchased the featured product category in the past year

In this case, all customers get the exact same score and look identical in terms of their likelihood to respond. Let's assume they all score 0.62. Any marketing program based on this model will treat each of these four customers the same. After all, based on the preceding information, nothing differentiates them; they are exactly the same!

Now, using web data, let's see how drastically the view changes. Look how the web data provides powerful new information:

- Customer 1 has never browsed your site, so his score drops to 0.54.
- Customer 2 viewed the product category featured in the offer within the past month, so her score rises to 0.67.
- Customer 3 viewed the specific product featured in the offer within the past month, so his score rises to 0.78.
- Customer 4 browsed the specific product featured three times last week, added it to a basket once, abandoned the basket, and then viewed the product again later. Her score rises to 0.86.

This web behavior allows us to identify customers with a current interest, if not intention, to purchase. It is possible to score customers better and end up with solid differentiation among them, where originally there was none. Now, repeat the example of these four customers across millions of customers across multiple channels, and dramatic changes can be driven!

When asked about the value of incorporating web data, a director of marketing from a multichannel American specialty retailer replied, "It's like printing money!" The good news is that it is very easy to build a model both with and without web data to prove exactly how results improve for any given situation. There is virtually no risk in testing the impact in your organization's environment.

Customer Segmentation

Web data also enables a variety of completely new analytics. One of those is to segment customers based solely on their typical browsing patterns. Such segmentation provides a completely different view of customers than traditional demographic or sales-based segmentation schemas. In addition, such segmentation can yield unique insights and actions.

Consider a segment called Dreamers that has been derived purely from browsing behavior. Dreamers repeatedly put an item in their baskets but then abandon them. Dreamers often add and abandon the same item many times. This may be especially true of high-value items such as TVs and computers. It isn't difficult to clearly identify the segment of people who do this repeatedly. So what can you do after finding them?

One option is to look at what the customers are abandoning. Perhaps a customer is looking at a high-end TV that is quite expensive. You've seen in the past that this customer often aims too high and eventually buys a less-expensive product than the one she abandoned repeatedly. Sending her an email pointing out less-expensive products that have many of the same features may be a way to get her to buy a TV sooner.

New Analytics Arise from Web Data

A variety of data sources are used for customer segmentation. Sales, demographics, and survey responses are some of them. It is now possible to segment customers according to their browsing behavior as well. This provides insight into customers' shopping styles and thought processes and is a terrific additional dimension to add to your mix of segmentation criteria.

Another option is operational in nature. Abandoned-basket statistics can be adjusted to account for the Dreamer segment. Organizations often view abandoned baskets as a failure. However, by examining the browsing history, you find that 10 abandons were from one customer who is known to repeatedly and regularly abandon many products. As a result, the abandoned-basket count can be reduced, and all the customer's abandons for that product can be counted as a single abandonment. This yields a cleaner view of abandonment. By the time statistics are adjusted for all such customers, the average abandonment rate might look quite a bit better. Not only do the new figures look better, but they also are a more accurate reflection of reality.

Assessing Advertising Results

Better assessing paid search and online advertising results is another high-impact analysis enabled with customer-level web behavior data. Traditional web analytics provide high-level summaries such as total clicks, number of searches, cost per click or impression, keywords leading to the most clicks, and page position statistics. However, these metrics are at an aggregate level and are rolled up only from the individual browsing session level. The context is limited solely to the web channel.

This means that all statistics are based only on what happened during the single session generated from the search or ad click. When a customer leaves the website and his web session ends, the scope of the analysis is complete. There is no attempt to account for past or future visits in the statistics. By incorporating customers' browsing data and extending the view to other channels as well, it is possible to assess search and advertising results at a much deeper level.

- Were the site visits each ad or search term generated associated with the most valuable or least valuable customers?
- How many sales did the initial session lead to in the days or weeks that followed the customer's first click?
- Are certain referring websites drawing visitors who return for more visits and make more total purchases than visitors referred from other sites?
- By doing a cross-channel analysis that accounts for activity in other channels, are a lot of sales closed in a second channel after interest is generated on the Web via an ad or search?

Let's consider an example from a financial institution. Credit card applications are everywhere. They are in the mail, they are in magazines, and they are available all over the Web. The bank in our example understands that "eyeballs and clicks" are only a portion of the picture. What happens after the initial click is the telling information about the value of an advertising placement.

The bank performs extensive analytics to dive deeper and look at more than just clicks from the initial session. Customers are examined across time and sessions to also assess application completion, customer service inquiries, card issuance, card activation, and initial credit spending. This view of advertising beyond the click provides a more complete view of advertising success and leads to smarter allocation of advertising budgets.

Why Limit Yourself to the Immediate?

Identifying the outcome of a web session started with an advertisement, email click, or search misses the mark. Many customers will come back later to finish what they started, perhaps even in a different channel. Traditional web analytics do not account for future behavior after an initial session; nor do they account for historical behavior that happened prior to the session. Upgrade your capabilities to allow you to do both.

Through detailed, customer-level web data, you can understand which ads, keywords, or referring sites generate the "best" clicks based on a much larger picture than simply aggregated results from initial web sessions. With the additional insight provided by the extended cross-channel, cross-time view, you can see a picture that has previously been unavailable. Organizations that understand the deeper context will have an opportunity to take advantage of new strategies that those using traditional levels of analysis will be unable to identify. That is a distinct competitive advantage.

Wrap-Up

Here are the most important lessons to take away from this chapter:

- The integration of detailed, customer-level web behavior data can transform what organizations understand about their customers.

- Just as transactional data enabled a revolution in the power and depth of analysis when it became available, so will web data allow you to take analytics to a new level.

- Other customer touchpoints can be tracked in a similar fashion as a website, such as kiosks and mobile phone applications. The same principles apply.

- Any data that can be captured should be. This includes page views, searches, downloads, and any other activity on a website.

- Privacy is a major concern with web data, so you should be careful when defining policies on how such data will be used. Those policies must be rigorously followed and enforced.

- You can generate tremendous value by analyzing faceless customers who are identified only by an arbitrary identification number. This way, neither analysts nor anyone else can identify who each customer actually is. Only the patterns matter.

- Web data helps you understand detailed customer shopping, research, and feedback behaviors and purchase paths. It is almost as if you can read your customers' minds.

- Web data enables stronger results in areas such as next best offer, attrition modeling, response modeling, customer segmentation, paid search, and online advertising analysis.
- The opportunity to be an early adopter and get ahead of the competition is almost over. Get started taming this big-data source now!

5

The Analytics of Online Engagement

Eric T. Peterson

Engagement of customers with online resources is an important but elusive concept. Companies have struggled with the meaning and measurement of online engagement for years. However, none of the common website metrics—page views, clicks, surveys, time spent, conversions, loyalty—is an acceptable proxy for engagement.

To make engagement more understandable and actionable, my firm, Web Analytics Demystified, Inc., has developed both a definition and a framework that reduces a wide variety of website metrics to a single visitor-engagement score. Once calculated, this score can be used to segment visitors for a variety of purposes, such as digital marketing, content improvement, keyword enhancement, and partnership development.

The Definition of Engagement

Because *engagement* can mean different things to different people, it has proven to be a frustrating metric for businesses to nail down. Some equate it with online activity, others focus on loyalty, and still others emphasize conversion rates. But each of these metrics fails to comprehensively support analytical decision-making. Based on observing various approaches, the following points seem clear:

- **Engagement isn't conversion.** Conversion (going from browsing to buying) looks at those who purchase, but it ignores the vast majority who don't. Just because a person doesn't buy online, does that mean he or she isn't engaged? What characterizes the online behavior of the "unconverted?" How can a company better reach them for later conversion? Conversion is undoubtedly a type of engagement, but it's not the whole story. For example, someone may spend hours on the Porsche website, but just because he doesn't purchase a Porsche online (which is rare) doesn't mean he isn't engaged. There is also the need to measure engagement with sites that offer only content and no opportunity to purchase anything.

- **Engagement isn't activity.** Average time spent, page views, and clicks per visit certainly capture web activity, but to what end? Are more page views and clicks necessarily better? Could clicks be the result of frustration rather than interest? Who is "average," anyway?

- **Engagement isn't satisfaction.** Although qualitative customer satisfaction (via tools from iPerceptions and ForeSee) and loyalty (embodied in metrics such as the Net Promoter Score) are both useful to track, neither says much about engagement. For example, a customer can simultaneously be highly dissatisfied and highly engaged in complaining about a brand on social networks. It is critical to measure both.

No one metric of engagement has emerged because of all the confusion surrounding the meaning of the concept.

Due to this uncertainty and lack of a consensus metric, approaches attempting to measure engagement have proliferated. In a recent poll, organizations reported using these approaches, among others:

- Traditional web analytics: 51%
- Online surveys: 34%
- Customer journey analytics: 30%
- Feedback from customer-facing staff: 28%
- Customer interviews: 27%

To be clear, all of these are worthwhile inputs, and companies should continue gathering and studying them. But none provides a complete picture of engagement.

Other organizations have attempted to define engagement, but not in a way that lends itself to analytical measurement and action:

- **Forrester Research:** "Engagement is the level of involvement, interaction, intimacy, and influence an individual has with a brand over time."
- **Advertising Research Foundation (ARF):** "Engagement is turning on a prospect to a brand idea enhanced by the surrounding context."

Both of these definitions have some appeal, but they would be difficult to translate into metrics in an offline context.

In 2007, Web Analytics Demystified, Inc. took its first pass at a more useful definition:

> Engagement is an estimate of the degree and depth of visitor interaction against a clearly defined set of goals.

The inclusion of *goals* in the definition gives it teeth and provides a linkage to action. To even begin to measure engagement, a business must identify what actions it wants visitors to take on its site. Download a paper? Watch a video? Join a forum? Subscribe to a newsletter? Buy something? Fill out a contact form? Prioritizing a particular task or task set implies data and measurement.

Feeling that our definition still lacked precision, in 2008 we released this revised version:

> Engagement is the *demonstration* of *Attention* via psychomotor activity that serves to focus an individual's Attention. Attention is a behavior that demonstrates that specific neural activity is taking place.

The stress on *attention* is intentional: In this definition, engagement is seen not as an external activity but as an internal mental state, something happening in the brain. Terms such as *psychomotor* and *neural* puzzled clients and other interested parties, however, so the third version blended the best of both:

> Engagement is an estimate of the depth of visitor interaction against a clearly defined set of goals. Demonstrated Attention is measured via "visitor interaction."

A Model to Measure Online Engagement

To put the definition to work, the company developed a robust but flexible framework that captures multiple aspects of visitor interaction, as shown in Figure 5.1. We have updated it over time to add missing components.

$$\sum_{\text{Visitor}} (C_i + R_i + D_i + L_i + B_i + F_i + I_i + S_i)$$

Figure 5.1 Measuring online engagement.

Before we get into the details of the model, it is important to remember that this is a general model, not an optimized calculation for all types of sites. I agree with other analysts and bloggers who insightfully say that no single calculation of engagement is useful for all sites. But I do believe that this model is robust and useful with only slight modification across a wide range of sites. The modification comes in the thresholds for individual indices, the qualitative component, and the measured events, as discussed next. Otherwise, I believe that any site capable of making this calculation can do so without having to rethink the entire model.

The calculation of engagement using this model needs to be made over the lifetime of visitor sessions to the site and needs to accommodate different time spans. This means that to calculate the percentage of sessions having more than five page views, you need to examine *all the visitor's sessions during the time frame under examination* and determine which had more than five page views. If the calculation is unbounded by time, you would examine *all* of the visitor's sessions in the available dataset. If the calculation was bounded by the last 90 days, you would examine sessions *only* during the past 90 days.

The individual session-based indices are defined as follows:

- **Click-Depth Index (C_i)** is the percentage of sessions having more than n page views divided by all sessions. (The calculation of n is discussed in a moment.)
- **Recency Index (R_i)** is the percentage of sessions having more than n page views *that occurred in the past n weeks* divided by

all sessions. The recency index captures recent sessions that are also deep enough to be measured in the Click-Depth Index.

- **Duration Index (D**i**)** is the percentage of sessions longer than n minutes divided by all sessions.

- **Brand Index (B**i**)** is the percentage of sessions that either began directly (had no referring URL) or were initiated by an external search for a "branded" term divided by all sessions.

- **Feedback Index (F**i**)** is the percentage of sessions where the visitor gave direct feedback via a Voice of the Customer technology such as ForeSee Results or OpinionLab, divided by all sessions.

- **Interaction Index (I**i**)** is the percentage of sessions where the visitor completed one of any specific, tracked events divided by all sessions.

In addition to the session-based indices, I have added two small, binary *weighting factors* based on visitor behavior:

- **Loyalty Index (L**i**)** is scored as 1 if the visitor has come to the site more than n times during the time frame under examination. Otherwise, it is scored 0.

- **Subscription Index (S**i**)** is scored as 1 if the visitor is a known content subscriber (subscribed to my blog) during the time frame under examination. Otherwise, it is scored 0.

In each component of the index, the n value is arbitrary, but new users are encouraged to use their particular site's averages to represent n. In other words, if a site's average number of page views is six, a visitor who views eight pages is assigned a 1 for that index, and a visitor who views three is given a 0 score. (Later, more experienced users can separately weight each index.) Calculate the overall engagement score by summing the component values, dividing by 7, and converting that number (which will be between 0 and 1) into a percentage. (For a more complete description of the model, as well as free ebook and whitepaper downloads, visit www.webanalyticsdemystified.com.)

To create the overall engagement score, take the value of each component index, sum them, and divide by 8 (the total number of indices in my model) to get a clean value between 0 and 1 that is easily converted into a percentage.

The Value of Engagement Scores

Once visitors have been scored, it is a straightforward matter to segment them into categories such as "highly engaged," "somewhat engaged," and "poorly engaged." These segments become useful key performance indicators (KPIs) when added to current site reports. Note that this metric doesn't judge whether a particular visitor is happy or sad, satisfied or dissatisfied, or can find what he or she is looking for. It simply makes a reasonable assumption that the visitor is paying attention, which is Web Analytics Demystified, Inc.'s proxy for engagement.

Although high-end software solutions such as Adobe's SiteCatalyst, IBM's Coremetrics, and Webtrends' Analytics are potent tools, even a free product such as Google Analytics can produce significant insights from this sort of enhanced data.

With a "poorly engaged" segment defined, for example, a site owner can examine reports to answer questions such as these:

- On which *landing pages* did this segment arrive?
- From which *search engines* did they come? What *search terms* did they use?
- What did they *buy*?
- To what *digital marketing* did they respond? Based on their subsequent purchases, was it cost-effective?
- From which *countries* are they coming? For business-to-business (B2B) entities, from which *domains*?

Also, from these insights come potential actions:

- **Changing site content.** What else could we be doing for our highly engaged visitors? How should we be treating them to move the conversation toward a task or goal?
- **Learning from clickthrough referrers.** Ask them these questions: What do our engaged visitors click at your site? How can we help you send more of this segment to us? Should we provide the highly engaged who click through with different content opportunities?
- **Analyzing keywords.** An analysis of search phrases that a segment uses may suggest the purchase of new, nonobvious, and

more cost-effective terms at search sites. The use of branded keywords is an explicit illustration of attention as a mental state.

• **Triggering alerts.** When a visitor's engagement score suddenly spikes—say, from 30% to 60%—this may signal an imminent purchase decision, particularly in a B2B environment. A triggered report could prompt a salesperson to pick up the phone and call the prospect.

Perhaps the best way to illustrate the use of the model is to describe its application in two organizations: PBS and Philly.com. Both organizations were able to make substantial improvements in their online results after switching to engagement-oriented metrics and analyses.

Engagement Analytics at PBS

PBS is a private, nonprofit corporation founded in 1969. Its members are America's public television stations—noncommercial, educational licensees that operate nearly 360 PBS member stations and serve all 50 states, Puerto Rico, U.S. Virgin Islands, Guam, and American Samoa. The corporation has transformed itself from a broadcast-only model to a truly multiplatform leader that serves Americans through television, mobile TV, the Web, interactive classrooms, and more. PBS reaches almost 117 million people through television and nearly 20 million people online each month.

The shift online has created entirely new opportunities with the corporation's consumer audience. One of these opportunities is applying new, digital analytical applications to create a more robust understanding of audience engagement with properties, shows, technologies, and campaigns. Given the relatively high volume of consumer data generated by the corporation's multiple digital investments, conventional wisdom dictated that developing this understanding of the online consumer could positively impact PBS's programming strategy, both online and offline.

In 2009, under the direction of Jason Seiken, Senior Vice President of PBS Interactive, Amy Sample, Director of Web Analytics, set out to implement a multifaceted measure of engagement. It leveraged the corporation's investments in web analytics technology. This measure was incorporated into PBS's existing analytics efforts and ultimately was used to help the corporation grow audience and revenue and increase engagement and satisfaction. According to Sample, "Understanding and measuring user engagement with our content has advanced our use of analytics at PBS beyond just audience reason and page views. By focusing on engagement with our content, we are delivering better experiences for our users."

PBS uses Google's Google Analytics offering to measure and analyze its online audiences. Although it isn't as powerful or sophisticated as other available tools, Google Analytics provided Sample and her team two benefits that ultimately drove the effort's success:

- A user interface to the data that led the industry in terms of simplicity
- A set of application programming interfaces (APIs) that allowed the engagement data to be pulled into the corporation's wider reporting efforts

The engagement calculation that Sample ended up using leveraged measures of audience loyalty, recency of visit, visit duration, and depth of visit. It was largely based on work done by Web Analytics Demystified and Victor Acquah, a consultant working for PBS. Through experimentation, Sample and Acquah determined that different combinations of this data were required, depending on which site was being measured, primarily because of the diversity of audiences the corporation serves.

Since rolling the measure of engagement out across PBS digital properties in 2010, the conversation has shifted. The debate used to be over "what engagement means" and "how engagement should be measured." Now it is "which of PBS's digital efforts drive online engagement," "how engagement can be increased," and "what impact increasing engagement has on satisfaction, audience composition, and ultimately revenue." Moreover, Sample can compare engagement profiles across multiple PBS digital properties and investments, focusing on which engagement efforts are working and which need additional attention.

Sample and Acquah continue to analyze the drivers of engagement on PBS properties. Through their analysis, they discovered that video is a key driver of user engagement on PBS.org. As a result of their analysis, video content was featured more prominently on the redesigned home page, leading to a 42% increase in monthly video views. This translated into hundreds of thousands of dollars in incremental sponsor-driven revenue for PBS. "We have substantially grown our video streams and overall traffic by being very metrics-driven," says Seiken. "The numbers confirm that we are keeping consumers engaged longer and dispelling the myth that PBS is just for older generations. The combination of our engagement analysis and our unique, uncluttered environment increases our potential sponsorship revenue."

For 2011, PBS established a goal of increasing the total number of engaged users visiting PBS websites by 8 to 10 percent. The logic is, of course, that your best customers are your existing customers, but if you cannot keep those customers engaged you may lose them. Further, as the advertising community continues to examine their investments (and as PBS further explores advertising-based revenue models), having a good story to tell about the quantity and the quality of the PBS audience only helps drive revenue.

Engagement Analytics at Philly.com

Philly.com is an award-winning news, sports, and commentary site. It is the online home of the *Philadelphia Inquirer* and *Philadelphia Daily News*. It also creates a significant amount of its own content and aggregates the work of quality partners in the Philadelphia area. The site is particularly strong in breaking news and sports, which make up 30% to 40% of overall site traffic. Philly.com has been aggressive in adding new user engagement features, including gaming in sports and reader chats. It operates a professional video unit that produces about eight video shows per week. In 2009, the site was named a Top 10 sports news site in the country by the Associated Press Sports Editors. In 2011, the site won second place in the prestigious national Headliner Awards among newspaper websites for online presentation of a special report.

In early 2010, at the suggestion of the company's web analytics manager, Chris Meares, leadership at Philly.com began exploring the use of visitor engagement as an alternative to traditional, page view-based measures of success on the site. Meares was familiar with the indices described in this chapter, and he determined how each could best be used for sales, marketing, and content planning purposes. He presented his results to the then-President, Vice President of Content, Vice President of Product Development, and Vice President of Sales.

Under the direction of Kevin Stetter, Vice President of Advertising, Meares set about creating a single measure of visitor engagement using Omniture SiteCatalyst and Omniture Discover. This metric, a variant on the model described earlier, was hashed out through trial and error against the key segments that the company had already been tracking. Initially, when Meares presented the finished product to the Sales organization, some concern arose, primarily from the perceived complexity of the calculation when compared to the company's relatively simple existing set of metrics. However, as soon as Meares and Stetter explained the work behind the measure of visitor engagement, Sales immediately warmed to the idea, especially when they realized they would be able to sell advertisers on more engaged audiences and more engaging sections of the site.

Product managers and other content owners started using the visitor engagement metric as well, applying the calculation to different site sections, referring traffic sources, and geographic targeting data. What's more, insights derived from the measure were found immediately and impacted multiple areas of the site, including jobs and real estate. Meares also discovered a strong correlation between sports content and engagement across the entire site that is now leveraged as an "early warning system" to predict when overall site traffic (and thus advertising-based revenue) is waxing or waning. Now, as opposed to page views and visits, visitor engagement is the measure of success against which the Vice Presidents of Content and Product hold their staffs accountable.

"Needing a new online metric that focused more on the content of our website and geared toward our loyal visitors, Philly.com moved to engagement as the measuring stick for the performance of our website," said Meares. "Since we have become more focused on driving the engagement of our visitors, we have seen an overall increase in content-related page views of over 26%, which is our most valuable inventory for advertising sales." What's more, analysis predicts that revenues derived from incremental advertising sales will be as much as 10%, an estimated $500,000 to $650,000 per year.

Additionally, the company's visitor engagement efforts have positively impacted many of the company's valuable partnerships. "Since we instituted the engagement metric at Philly.com and moved away from tracking just page views and visits, we have learned much more about our most loyal users," said Stetter. "The engagement metric has proved invaluable when discussing new online strategic initiatives as well as evaluating the current partnerships on our site. We are now able to gauge the effectiveness of our current and future partnerships from an engaged audience standpoint, which then allows us to tell a unique story to our advertisers."

Thanks to a particularly good use of Adobe's Omniture technology, a motivated analyst in Chris Meares, and a group of forward-thinking executives including Kevin Stetter, Philly.com is well positioned from advertising sales, partnership, and editorial perspectives. Over time, the measure of visitor engagement is likely to evolve in both its calculation and use to deliver increasingly valuable insights.

6

The Path to "Next Best Offers" for Retail Customers

Thomas H. Davenport, John Lucker, and Leandro DalleMule

Retailers hunger for new, effective ways to drive sales, traffic, and growth for their stores, sites, catalogs, and other channels. In the past, they relied on local salespeople to match the right products to the right customers and to suggest the perfect offer to motivate a sale. Today, multiple customer channels, shorthanded staff, and busy consumers are driving innovative mechanisms for *next best offers*, using data analysis and technology to enable scalable precision. Next best offers also have relevance for any other industry with consumers as customers, including consumer financial services, travel and transportation, and telecommunications.

The "next best offer" (NBO) is a targeted offer or proposed action for customers based on the following:

- Analyses of their past shopping history and behavior
- Other customer preferences, attributes, and life stages
- Purchasing context
- Attributes of the products or services from which they can choose

NBOs should result in a high likelihood of purchase, but the best programs go beyond the sales transaction. They reward the customer for past loyalty, deepen an existing customer relationship, and appeal in a highly relevant way.

NBOs tend to apply particularly to companies providing services directly to consumers; business-to-business firms may not have enough data to draw on. Offers can consist of products and service discounts (diaper or spa treatment coupons), information (Google ads to click), or even relationships (LinkedIn and Facebook recommendations). They may be delivered through in-store salespeople, call centers, direct mail, kiosks, register receipts, and mobile devices.

Clearly, well-designed NBOs are the future of retailing; presently, however, NBOs are either poorly executed or not done at all. Most offers are indiscriminate, ill-targeted, and too numerous—the new junk mail. One major retail bank concluded that its offers were more likely to create ill will than increases in sales.

Analytics and the Path to Effective Next Best Offers

The world of customer analytics is a complex and fast-changing one with incredible potential. This is the process by which data from customer behavior is applied to key business decisions via market segmentation and predictive analytics. NBO programs are a worthy target for any company wanting to develop or improve its use of data and analytics to serve customers, because they require knowledge of customers, products, offers, and the rules and algorithms for combining them.

No organization today has "mastered" NBOs, but some have made dramatic progress toward creating offers that do the following:

- Meet the company's objectives
- Are targeted to a customer segment of one
- Arrive via the customer's preferred channel
- Are delivered when the customer is in the mood and location to buy
- Have a high conversion rate that can be achieved and measured
- Take into account the customer's life stage, previous buying behavior, current location, and all responses to previous offers
- Incorporate the discussions and behaviors of friends in social media

Short of the perfect offer, there is still substantial opportunity to create and improve NBOs. In our research, we've created a framework for effective NBO initiatives, as shown in Figure 6.1. Some companies may not be ready to undertake all these steps at once, but eventual progress in each phase will be necessary to improve offers.

Figure 6.1 The path to next best offers.

Offer Strategy Design

As with any strategy, an organization should begin by reflecting on what it wants to accomplish with its offers and how those goals can best be achieved. Offer strategy design should include topics such as these:

- How you want offers to affect your customer relationship
- What channels you plan to use and under what circumstances
- What data to gather and analyze
- What you plan to offer
- How an offer may impact the market and competition

- Collaboration with manufacturers that supply products and finance offers

The U.K.-based retailer Tesco has been very successful with its targeted coupon offers in its loyalty program, Clubcard. But critical to the design of the offers program was Tesco's unrelenting desire to both know more about its customers' preferences than anyone else and to reward customer loyalty and other desired behaviors with coupons that they will welcome and try. The offers generated by Tesco and its in-house consultant, dunnhumby, achieve redemption rates averaging between 8% and 14%. This is far higher than the rest of the grocery industry, which averages between 1% and 2%. dunnhumby's research suggests that offers targeting loyal customers lead to higher revenue lift as well.

Microsoft's recent consumer offer campaign for Bing, its new search engine, focused on getting users to try Bing or use it more frequently. The company's marketers wanted to make the offers via email, but because the company sells email applications and is an avowed foe of spam, the offers needed to be perceived as highly relevant rather than invasive. So Microsoft employed a new technology, Infor's Interaction Advisor, for real-time targeted emails in the very successful campaign.

The objective for offers may well change over time. For example, the DVD rental firm Redbox initially made email- and kiosk-based offers with the objective of having customers try its rentals. In the process, customers got used to renting through the Redbox channel in a familiar, convenient location that the customer had to visit anyway (often grocery stores). The Redbox technical process required a learning curve for checkout and check-in. As the business grew, executives realized that more revenue and profit growth would result from offers encouraging customers to rent more than one DVD per visit.

It's just as important to declare what *not* to pursue in offers. One retail chain concluded that social media was not an important factor in determining offer content. The company's marketing analysts monitored social media content about the company and observed that the products it sells are not a major focus of discussion. For Ticketmaster, however, there is little doubt that social media play an important role in young customers' decisions about what concerts and events to attend. Therefore, analyzing social media and using it as a delivery channel will be increasingly important to its offers.

Know Your Customer

Targeted offers are based on the detailed analysis of information about the customer, product offering, and purchase context. Customer information can include basic attributes such as demographics, residence, previous purchases, income, and assets. From these raw information sources, a vast trove of synthetic data can be created by combining like and disparate fields in meaningful ways—ratios, statistically derived fields, and derivations of averages and probabilities. Some of these fields are readily available, but others can be difficult to obtain and integrate with other customer data. In addition, new possibilities for customer information are opening up through "SoMoLo" (social, mobile, location) data:

- Where is the customer at this moment—anywhere near one of my stores?
- What is the customer saying about my company or brands in social media, and how influential is he?
- What are my customers' friends buying and discussing online?

Walmart acquired the start-up Kosmix to begin employing SoMoLo data in its offers. The apparel retailer H&M created a partnership with the online gaming firm MyTown to gather and use information on customer location. If a potential customer is playing the game on a mobile device near an H&M store, H&M makes offers of items to be used in the game. Customers are encouraged to go into the store and scan the item for a discount. Early results suggested that, out of 700,000 online check-ins by customers, 300,000 went into the store and scanned an item.

Know Your Offers

Many companies overlook the fact that they also need accurate product information and attributes to succeed with NBOs. There must be a sound basis for matching a customer and a product based on customer-specific, appealing product attributes.

For some products, product attributes can easily be obtained from third-party databases. For example, firms making movie offers (including Netflix, AT&T, and Comcast) can surmise that if you liked one movie with a particular actor or plot type, you will probably like another. But for other retail industries, such as apparel and grocery retailing, compiling product attributes is much more difficult. Manufacturers don't have official classifications of whether a sweater is "fashion-forward" or "traditional." Grocery retailers can't easily determine what food products appeal to customers with adventurous, healthy, or penny-pinching tastes.

It's also important to know what products manufacturers want to promote and what their objectives are for the customer's product use. Do they want customers to try it, acquire more of it, or perhaps buy it in combination with another product?

Tesco has aggressively pursued the classification of product attributes to ensure that customers receive offers related to their tastes. Attributes, such as whether a product is frozen or not, or the cost per kilogram, are sourced from its product databases. But for those involving taste and lifestyle, which are more difficult to classify, Tesco employs a "rolling snowball" approach to identifying taste-related product attributes. For example, to identify products that appeal to adventurous palates, it takes a product that is widely agreed to be adventurous in a country context. In the U.K., Tesco chose Thai green curry paste and identified other adventurous products by analyzing relatedness coefficients. If customers who bought curry paste also bought squid and wild rocket (arugula) pesto, these products probably appeal to adventurous customers.

Know the Purchase Context

Offers should also be based on a variety of purchase context factors, such as the inbound channel for customer contact. Did it occur by walk-in, telephone, email, web browser, receiving mass media messages? Online offers can be based on a variety of immediately preceding behaviors, including the previous site visited and click-streams on the company's own site. The customer's reason for contact is another important variable. Is he or she shopping for someone else, seeking service, carrying out another transaction, seeking offers, or simply minding his or her own business?

Other contextual factors might include the time of day, current weather, and whether the customer is alone or accompanied. One Chinese shoe retailer has developed offers that target companion shoppers. When a woman walks in the store with her husband, this retailer offers him a relatively inexpensive item. The decision of which item to offer the husband is heavily based on his higher price sensitivity as a companion, versus his lower sensitivity when shopping for himself.

Some of the most valuable purchase context information today comes in the form of SoMoLo data. With proper usage, retailers can develop a ubiquitous capability to offer products and enhance the customer experience. Social and mobile data channels the voice of the consumer and many aspects of his or her preferences and behaviors, telling retailers what offers are more likely to succeed and when.

An interesting application of social data to develop highly customized offers comes from Sony, which has been experimenting with Facebook Connect, a tool that allows Facebook members to take their social networks with them around the Internet. Sony plans to use Connect to enable its developers to create personalized video game offers on the PlayStation 3 console. Game developers can pull information out of Facebook and push information to it. The next generation of video game offers could have pictures of your friends or your tastes and interests built right in.

If appropriately analyzed, mobile data also can help you better understand customer preferences, needs, and desires, and significantly enhance retailers' ability to design their NBOs. Many retailers are focused on immediate location, which is valuable in targeting customers who have a strong propensity to buy. But location history can reveal a lot about customers as well. A company called Sense Networks has developed an application to help infer a person's lifestyle based on his or her location history. Sense Networks claims it can estimate customer attributes such as age, probability of being a business traveler, wealth, and next likely location. By comparing where targeted customers go against data points on the movements of other customers, the company can create granular segments and allow retailers to offer targeted, timely NBOs.

Analytics and Execution: Deciding on and Making the Offer

NBOs are created by a predictive model or test, based on a series of variables or attributes. The goal is to identify the attributes most related to specific, desired customer propensities, actions, and outcomes. Simple predictive NBOs, such as those offered initially by Amazon.com, with "people who bought this may also buy that" cross-purchase correlations, don't employ substantial knowledge of the customer or product attributes. In addition, Amazon makes email-based NBOs based on past purchase behavior. Unfortunately, if a customer buys something for a friend, he might be stuck with irrelevant offers for years.

Personalized offers normally are based on a combination of algorithms predicting a customer's probabilistic propensity to purchase, customer lifetime value, cross-sell and up-sell probabilities, and business rules governing what offers are made under what circumstances. For example, a business rule might determine what offer is made when several products have equal propensity scores or might limit the overall contact frequency for a customer.

A key aspect of offer execution is to decide how and by whom the offer is to be delivered. The outbound mode of delivery of the offer is usually the same as the inbound channel, but not always. It can include

- Face-to-face outreach by a human
- In-store kiosk
- Mobile device
- Online: email or banner ad
- Register receipt
- Mass media

Many companies are attempting to address offers through multiple channels. "Our customers never met a channel they didn't like," said a retail banking executive. At CVS, the company's ExtraCare loyalty program offers are delivered through register receipts, in-store kiosks, email, and even targeted circulars, and the company is experimenting with mobile coupons. Qdoba Mexican Grill, a quick-serve franchise, is using mobile coupons to expand its card-based loyalty program. It can deliver offers at certain times to increase traffic, while smoothing demand during peak times. Late-night campaigns near universities have seen a 40% redemption rate, while the average redemption rate is 16% for the whole program.

Starbucks uses over 11 online channels to develop targeted offers, gauge customer satisfaction and reaction, develop products, and enhance brand advocacy. Today more than 30 million Facebook users "like" Starbucks, more than 2 million follow the retailer on Twitter, and more than 300,000 images with Starbucks tags were uploaded to Flickr. Facebook fans spend on average $235 per year at Starbucks— more than twice the amount that nonfans spend. These fans comprise a loyal affinity group with strong purchase propensities. The company also uses location-based services such as Foursquare to offer rewards to customers for brand advocacy. Its smartphone app allows customers to opt in to messages based on age, gender, interests, and location, which enables Starbucks to tailor promotions to specific audiences.

Some upscale retailers, such as Nordstrom, and financial services firms serving wealthy customers believe that the best channel for delivering an offer is a human being. Many organizations provide multiple offers, usually ranked by the customer's propensity to accept them. A salesperson can select an offer based on real-time perceived receptivity and comfort level with the client. When a salesperson delivers offers, a delicate interplay often occurs between the salesperson's perceptions of the customer and the offers presented by the model. Insisting that a salesperson deliver an offer in all cases may create lower satisfaction and reduced offer compliance. The investment firm T. Rowe Price estimates that its targeted offers shouldn't be delivered more than 50% of the time. Otherwise, the employee probably isn't tuning into what the customer really wants.

Online offers are less personal but can be sophisticated. Traditionally, online marketers have created a few different email offers and sent them to selected customer segments, and the offer is designed before the customer opens the message. However, sophisticated companies such as Microsoft are approaching offers much more dynamically. For example, emailed offers for trying or becoming more engaged with the Bing search engine are customized at the time of opening. In 200 milliseconds, a lag time imperceptible to customers, the offer is assembled based on the most recent responses of other customers and the available real-time information about the current customer. The real-time targeted ads have lifted conversion rates between 20% and 70% under different circumstances.

Given the richness, diversity, and inherent personal nature of much of the data used for NBOs, a large array of issues naturally emerge that touch on legal, ethical, political, and public policy concepts. These issues have largely been in the background thus far, but they are becoming more prominent. They address not just identity protection or privacy, but also how pervasive and invasive the offers can be as perceived by customers—the offers' mood, tone, and feel.

Here are some questions central to this topic:

- How might consumers be fairly or unfairly treated by NBOs?
- Are offers being made based on truthful and accurate information or erroneous and spurious data?
- Are consumers comfortable with offers that are derived from seemingly unrelated information and that make assumptions about propensities?
- Are consumers aware and accepting of evolving data usage capabilities, and can they opt into or out of future data usage techniques?
- How might a consumer react if an offer results in a "false positive" and the offer insults or somehow offends the person's sensibilities?

This abbreviated list of concerns includes some critical topics that need specific and holistic consideration. Some touch on highly technical and controversial legal regulations articulated in laws such as the Fair Credit Reporting Act (FCRA). Outside of the U.S., particularly in the EU, regulations limiting the use of consumer information for NBOs can be much more restrictive.

Learning from and Adapting NBOs

Because offer creation is an inexact, but constantly improving, science, one of the most important components of a successful NBO process is to learn from and adapt to results. Some offers will meet customer needs better than others, so there must be a way to measure and improve success, both in the aggregate and for individual customers. The best way to view NBOs, as a CVS executive noted, is "every offer is a test." If you don't constantly try out new variables, algorithms, and business rules, your offers won't get better.

One way to learn from offers is to articulate some rules of thumb that govern the creation of offers. These will differ for each company, and it's important to articulate them explicitly so that they can guide offers. Here are some rules of thumb we derived from our discussions with companies:

- Up-sell happens only face-to-face (U.S. retail bank).
- Only fashion-forward shoes are discussed through social media (FootLocker).
- Our customers like offers that provide discounts on the same things they have bought previously (CVS).
- Offering a substantial discount on relevant items in categories where we would like to earn our member's business creates incremental value for us and our suppliers (Sam's Club).
- Our offers should generally be provided directly through our customer's relationship to sales associates via face-to-face customer interactions supported by powerful predictive analytical tools at the point-of-sale (Nordstrom).
- Customers don't seek to buy banking services often, so we need to partner with other providers to build the relationship (European bank).

Rules of thumb should be based on data-driven and fact-based analyses, not on convention or lore. And they should be tested occasionally to ensure that they still apply.

The key to NBOs is progress and innovation through action. It would be very difficult for a retailer today to incorporate all the possible variables into an NBO model. But it certainly makes sense to gather and incorporate key variables, such as basic demographics and customer purchase history. Most retailers, in fact, need to accelerate their work in this area because customers are not impressed by the quality and value of offers thus far. Channels and predictive variables will continue to grow in number, so if next best offers aren't quickly improving and evolving, they will only fall further behind.

Part III
Technologies for Analytics

7

Applying Analytics at Production Scale

James Taylor

One of the most powerful uses of data mining and predictive analytics is to apply these techniques to operational, transactional systems. This means applying analytic models and results on a production scale—to all customers, for all products, and embedded in production transactions. Organizations that succeed in applying analytics at such a scale see tremendous results. The benefit of analytics is applied to every one of a large number of transactions for a powerful multiplicative effect. To make this possible, analytics must be augmented with a family of technologies called *automated decision systems* or *decision management systems*.

Some industries use data mining and predictive analytics widely in production systems, but most do not. Industries that use the credit risk of an individual consumer in their decision-making are the most well-established. Companies such as credit card issuers and mobile telecom service providers routinely automate decisions that rely on sophisticated predictive analytic models to predict consumer credit risk. In addition, a growing number of companies are using propensity and profitability models in marketing and customer treatment.

In all these cases, the analytic models are applied to critical decisions within a business process. The risk models are applied to help decide which products can be profitably sold to a particular consumer as part of the origination or onboarding process. The propensity models are applied to improve decisions such as what to cross-sell or up-sell a particular consumer during the customer service process. What they have in common is a focus on *decisions* within these processes and on the use of analytical insights to determine how best to make these decisions automatically, quickly, and accurately.

To succeed at using analytics in this way, however, organizations must address technology and organizational challenges that otherwise can derail these attempts. In particular, they must deal with organizational and attitudinal differences between business units, information technology (IT) departments, and analytics experts, as well as challenges involving compliance, time to deploy, and data consistency. These issues are described in this chapter. A detailed example of a company that has applied analytics successfully at production scale is then given.

Decisions Involve Actions

Data mining and predictive analytic techniques deliver insight for decisions. But decision-making also involves action: Making a decision involves making a commitment to taking a specific action. For analytical insight to improve decisions, it must result in the selection of a more profitable or otherwise "better" action. When analytical insight is delivered to human decision-makers, the expertise and know-how of those decision-makers can determine the appropriate action(s) from those available. When analytics are applied in a high-volume, low-latency production environment, typically no decision-maker is available. If humans are involved, they are unlikely to be qualified to make the decision; high-volume processes rarely employ experts, and those involved are likely to be junior staff. Even when humans are involved, they are there to deal with exceptions rather than routine decisions.

In either case, there is a need to formally define the available actions and to define how to select from among those actions so that the system can make the decision. The decision the system makes must use the predictions derived analytically, but it must also apply regulations, best practices, tribal knowledge, and company policies. For the decision to be made quickly and accurately, it must combine the analytic insight with the business rules—typically in an if/then format—that represent these policies and practices. Analytical insight alone is not enough.

Time to Business Impact

Analytical models, by their nature, tend to degrade over time. Analytical techniques typically are applied to a snapshot or extract of data from an organization's systems. Analyzing this data results in analytical insight, such as a prediction. When the prediction is made, it is accurate as of the time the data was extracted. When the delivery of an analytical model to a human decision-maker simply involves telling the person what the model said, there is little additional decay in the quality or accuracy of the model. When the model must be embedded into a production system, many additional steps might be necessary:

- Datasets used to build the analytical model may not match the data available in the production system, and this must be reconciled.

- The model must be applied to a whole series of transactions, often in real time. Therefore, the model's structure must be coded into an IT component that will execute the model against each transaction.

- As mentioned, the actions to be taken based on the model must be defined and likewise coded into an IT component. These are likely to change every time the model is updated, and it is common for them to change much more often than that.

- Although the model may already have been tested analytically, after it is deployed into an information system, it must be tested as an IT component.

All these steps take time. If they take too long, the model's accuracy and value will degrade before it can be put into production. In fact, if this process is difficult and too costly, the model will not make it into production and will never be used. In a recent survey I conducted, over 40% of organizations took more than six months to deploy models. Given that six months is also a typical time frame for updating a model, this implies that 40% of organizations are not getting a model into production before the analytical team would want to replace it with a new, more accurate model. Therefore, the time taken to deploy analytic models into production is critical.

In addition, the environment must be constantly monitored to ensure that the distribution and quality of data processed is as expected by the model and that the model's effectiveness does not degrade over time. Constant updates to the model are to be expected. If deploying a model is time-consuming and costly, updates will be impossible.

Business Decisions in Operation

When analytics are deployed into operational systems, organizational challenges arise. Anyone seeking to use analytics to improve decision-making must address the different ways in which business and analytical people think and talk. For example, an analytic model that cannot produce better business results may be interesting, but it is not useful. When analytic models are embedded in information systems, the IT department also must be able to participate.

This means more than just explaining the model. In the case of business people, the model must predict something they can use. For instance, predicting which consumers are a churn risk seven days before their contract expires is not useful in a business context where churning customers typically pick their new service provider 14 days before their contract expires.

In the case of IT people, the practical implications of implementing a model in the organization's IT environment must be taken into account. A model that is more accurate but requires more data sources or program interfaces—and therefore takes more time and money to implement—may be less valuable than a less-accurate model that can easily and quickly be put to work. Successful use of analytical insight in operational systems requires close and frequent cooperation between analytics, business, and IT people as models are being developed.

Compliance Issues

Because many of the decisions where analytics play a role in production systems and processes impact consumers, regulatory compliance is a real issue. Many decisions about consumers are regulated, often at multiple levels. This is especially true when it comes to applying risk models or when making pricing or eligibility decisions based, in part, on analytical insights. When a decision is regulated, the analytical team needs to consider how the model will be explained to regulators. Saying that a consumer was rejected or charged a higher price "because the model said so" is unlikely to be acceptable. Decisions with compliance issues need models that have explicable results. As a result, the use of techniques such as decision trees, association rules, and additive scorecards may be preferred over more opaque "black box" techniques, such as neural networks and machine learning.

Data Considerations

As noted, data issues arise when models are deployed into production around mapping the data available in production to the analytical datasets used to develop the models. This is not the only data issue that needs to be addressed, however. In addition, the three groups involved in implementing analytical production environments (business, IT, and analytics) all have quite different perspectives on data. IT departments typically think in terms of object models, of storing and managing data. Business users, meanwhile, see their data through the reports and dashboards they use to view it, often considering historical data only in terms of monthly or quarterly roll-ups. Analytical people tend to work with flat-file datasets and rarely use summary data, usually preferring raw transaction data in its full detail.

This difference in perspectives must be resolved when analytics are developed for use in production systems. Analytical and reporting data must be synchronized to ensure a common baseline for business and analytics teams. Analytics and IT departments must effectively manage the mapping of analytical data to production data sources.

Example of Analytics at Production Scale: YouSee

YouSee is Denmark's leading provider of cable TV and broadband services and aims to excel in terms of content, quality, and customer value. YouSee offers cable TV, IP telephony, mobile broadband, and digital TV services. In Denmark the company is first in digital TV market share, second in broadband, and third in telephony. YouSee's strategy includes developing an extended portfolio of HDTV and on-demand TV services and launching broadband services with speeds greater than 100Mbps. YouSee employs just over 1,200 people in Denmark and had revenues of 4.012 BDKK (US$775 million) in 2010. YouSee is a division of the TDC Group, Denmark, and was known as TDC Cable TV until it was spun off as an independent brand in 2007.

YouSee has a large number of cable TV customers—1.2 million households, representing approximately 46% of Danish households. Thirteen percent of these are YouSee Plus customers, paying for on-demand packages of TV shows and movies. Its broadband services reach 400,000 households and include web-based TV and the music service YouSee Play, with more than 10 million tracks. IP telephony reaches 69,000, and mobile broadband 3,000.

YouSee faced two challenges that were consistent with those of other telecom firms in other countries:

- Customers of TV and broadband products do not tend to be very loyal, so customer churn is a constant problem.
- Multiproduct customers are more profitable and more loyal, but many YouSee customers have only a single product.

These challenges were being exacerbated by new regulations that will allow competitors to sell broadband services over the YouSee cable network. Other organizations in Denmark are installing increas-ingly large fiber networks, and these too have the potential to offer competitive products. More competitors means more offers to con-sumers and therefore higher rates of churn.

With a strong leadership position in product innovation, YouSee identified customer service as a critical area of focus and its call center as the front line in its efforts to retain and develop customers.

Potential Solutions

YouSee believed that a 360-degree customer view would allow it to develop a solution that would generate additional sales and increase loyalty. The company hoped to take advantage of its many contact points with customers and effectively manage the customer dialog. A project to introduce predictive analytics to the call center was started. This project was sponsored at a high level by the president of sales and marketing due to its technical scope, importance to the business, and expected impact on customer handling.

The project involved a large number of people, both internal and external, and took approximately 14 months from start to go-live. Consultants participated in some elements of the project, but YouSee's internal IT and analytical departments took primary responsibility. The project was divided into technical and analytical infrastructure to develop predictive analytic models, and a Salesforce.com CRM implementation effort.

YouSee was clear on what it wanted to improve—the decision that a call center agent makes about a cross-sell or retention offer when talking to a customer. The company began with the belief that all customer data is relevant in addressing these problems. YouSee identified all the possible sources of information to build this rich customer view. Some 80 or 90 data sources were identified, with many containing data about a single product's customers.

Identifying all the data sources was a major effort because of the range of people who need to be involved to ensure completeness. Although the expertise required to identify and understand these data sources was largely internal, an industry-specific data model helped bring everything together. Not all this data is relevant to developing predictive analytic models, of course, but YouSee system designers believe that the models should determine what data is relevant.

The next step was to define and build an extract, transform, and load (ETL) process for these data sources. YouSee's IT department created an infrastructure for extracting the data from the original sources and loading it into what YouSee calls the Detailed Data Store. The Detailed Data Store contains all the data organized around a unique ID for every household, creating a 360-degree view of YouSee customers.

As soon as the Detailed Data Store was available, the analytics team created an analytical base table to support the development of predictive analytic models. This table takes all data collected and formats it to be suitable for analytic modeling. Data in the analytical base table is organized relative to dates when customers churned or made an additional product purchase. YouSee analysts hypothesized that the prior 180 days of historical data can predict the next 90 days, and this drives the data that is included.

Two initial models were then developed in SAS Enterprise Miner®, a data mining tool. For each broadband customer, the models deliver a probability (0 to 1) of a given event. The events are the likelihood of a successful cross-sell of cable TV services to a broadband subscriber in the next 90 days, and the likelihood that a broadband subscriber will churn in the next 90 days.

YouSee knew all along that simply displaying these predictive probabilities in the call center application would be unsatisfactory. Integrating the predictive analytic models into the call center CRM application involved two steps—making the predictive scores available to the application and then developing dynamic scripts that used those scores.

Deploying the predictive scores involved generating SAS code and running this code against the database every night to score each existing customer. Within the call center CRM system (Salesforce. com), YouSee created a set of business rules. These rules use the scores and many other data attributes to generate a suitable dynamic script for use with the customer. Only the most at-risk customers are selected. The business rules ensure that a customer doesn't get the same offer twice within a given period of time. Specific product campaigns override the models and manage eligibility of products based on the customer's location.

The combination of customer data, predictive models, and business rules decides what script the call center agents will see in Salesforce. Customers who are equally likely to churn will not necessarily get the same script because the script depends on their use of other services and other elements of their customer record. A unique "micro decision" is made for each customer to determine the best script.

The final stage of the project was maintenance and education. The models have to be monitored and updated when necessary, and the technical infrastructure also must be monitored constantly. In addition, the project educates and monitors the performance of call center agents.

YouSee Results

The implementation of dynamic and differentiated model-driven scripts has delivered an improvement in cross-sell and a reduction in churn for YouSee. Individual call center agents have achieved up to a 40% success rate on the cross-sell suggestions, for instance. Across the organization as a whole, a success rate of between 13% and 18% has been sustained even as usage rates have risen. The new scripts do contribute to a reduction in churn, but an exact number is difficult to estimate because several new set-top box and broadband services have been launched. These also influence customer churn.

The call center has changed its focus as a result of the solution. Script usage has risen steadily in the 18 months since the system went live. Some teams have much higher adoption than others—up to 3 times the teams with the lowest usage. The teams with supportive team leaders have higher adoption rates, which are strongly correlated to better sales numbers. Wait time and the time taken to handle a call are still key metrics, but the focus has now broadened to include retaining customers and selling them additional products.

With the solution deployed, the call center agents see only the scripts generated by the system. The agents don't see the predictions or necessarily know why a specific script has been generated. This allows even new, inexperienced agents and those with no analytic skills to use the predictive analytic models—truly pervasive analytics. In addition, YouSee now has a data warehouse for reporting and analysis purposes and has seen a big improvement in customer insight. In addition to the call center system, the CRM department as a whole is using the models to understand its customers and to help define campaigns. The product teams are also using the analytical results to help understand customers.

Challenges and Lessons Learned from YouSee

Getting to production scale from an IT and analytics perspective has been straightforward. The biggest challenge that YouSee faced in achieving the desired results was the human aspect of the solution. In particular, educating the call center agents on how the new system would work and why they should use it has been challenging.

In retrospect, the implementation team feels it spent too much time on IT and analytics and not enough time on the broader aspects of the business problem. In the 18 months since the system went live, usage has grown steadily. However it was not until 12 months after the system was first deployed that most of the teams reached an acceptable level of usage. Some teams are still struggling with adoption, but as a whole, usage levels are satisfactory.

Increasing the general understanding throughout YouSee of business analytics, including predictive analytic models and educating the call center agents, have been important tasks. Adoption and effective use of the solution remain an ongoing focus. The education of the call center agents needs to begin earlier in the project. The relatively high churn rate of call center agents also means that this education must be an ongoing task. Without this education, experienced agents prefer their "gut feelings" over the generated scripts. A number of initiatives are proving effective in this regard:

- Getting team leaders to spend more time on the solution has helped. Some teams have shown much higher usage and better results.

- Focusing on targets related to the solution (such as how often the scripts are used and their hit rate) has increased adoption.

- Comparing teams and showing that teams using scripts are outperforming those that do not has created internal competition and increased interest in the scripts.

- Hiring Salesforce quality consultants and instituting a Salesforce task force to increase adoption has had a positive impact.

- Using more dynamic scripts that are related to explicit campaigns known to the call center staff also has helped.

Because the solution requires a new interface in the call centers, change and adoption must be managed—After all, most people don't like change. The analytic team has also had to answer questions about how the predictive analytic models work to help those who must rely on the models trust them. Initial skepticism has given way to belief as the model-driven scripts have demonstrated their effectiveness.

The team has also found that it is essential to be able to continuously improve the decisions and the resulting scripts. Market conditions, competitors, and customer behavior are constantly evolving, and this leads to continuous change in data and conditions.

YouSee now knows that the first steps should have involved the call center and the call center agents more. An effort to develop and evolve the script interface and business rules in parallel with developing the predictive analytic models would have helped ensure more rapid adoption of the models when they were complete. Not involving the call center agents until a very late stage of the project resulted in a rough start to the "go-live" process.

Future Plans for Analytics at Scale

Three more churn and cross-sell models related to other YouSee products are in the development stage and will be used to drive additional scripts in the call center. Scripts are also being developed to see if a "next best action" approach should replace the current offer-centric approach. YouSee has some data to suggest that asking for email addresses and mobile phone numbers, so that more regular communication is possible in the future, might be more helpful in deepening the relationship with a customer than simply trying to sell something right now.

YouSee also plans to move to real-time scoring. In particular, the company plans to use real-time scoring to integrate predictive analytic model results into its web applications and set-top boxes. These boxes will allow its customers to rent movies and other content, and real-time scoring will support an analytically sophisticated recommendation engine. The current ad hoc use of the predictive analytic models to drive marketing campaigns will also be upgraded, using the models to drive systematic outbound campaigns.

Lessons Learned from Other Successful Companies

The issues YouSee faced are typical of those encountered by other organizations. These challenges are real and require different analytical development processes, organizational implementation techniques, and tools. There are certainly variations across different businesses and groups, but lessons can be learned from successful companies:

- Establish governance processes and technology to ensure that data used in analytical modeling will be available in production systems and reporting infrastructure. Do not allow these to get out of sync.

- Bring IT and business people into a multidisciplinary team early in the process. Do not allow the analytics team to work on the models alone.

- Invest early and consistently in teaching IT and business users the basics of analytics, especially what models can and cannot do.

- Ensure that your enterprise architecture contains an explicit description of how it will support decision-making IT components and the deployment of analytics. Don't allow decision-making components, or decision services as they are often called, to be treated like a generic IT component.

- Consider business rules management systems or applications with a strong business rules component as a deployment infrastructure for analytical models.

- Establish a separate IT life cycle and methodology for building, deploying, and evolving analytical decision-making components rather than using the standard IT software development life cycle.

- Focus on decisions. Ensure that you know which decisions are at issue, what their characteristics are, what their value is, and how they impact the company's business.

YouSee and other early adopters of production-scale analytics typically had to integrate products themselves and act without frameworks to support particular decisions at scale. More recently, however, companies that are well along in the use of decision technologies have begun to introduce the concept of "decision services" and have given them a role in their enterprise architectures.[1] In addition, business rules technology is increasingly being embedded within analytical systems. In the future, these previously separate worlds of business rules and analytical technology will increasingly be combined.

Endnote

1. For more on decision services, see James Taylor, *Decision Management Systems: A Practical Guide to Using Business Rules and Predictive Analytics*. Indianapolis: IBM Press, 2011.

8

Predictive Analytics in the Cloud

James Taylor

> "Innovation happens at the intersection of two or more different, yet similar, groups. Where one technology meets another, one discipline meets another, one department meets another."
>
> —*Valdis Krebs, Founder and Chief Scientist, orgnet.com*

Predictive analytics are increasingly the focus of many organizations' efforts to improve business performance. At the same time, the cloud is fast becoming an important option for purchasing and deploying software. Public, private, and hybrid clouds are all evolving rapidly and are here to stay. So what's happening at the intersection of these two technologies?

Over 200 professionals recently participated in a research study and survey of predictive analytics in the cloud conducted by Decision Management Solutions and Smart Data Collective.[1] Respondents came from organizations of all sizes. Over half were from organizations with fewer than 500 employees. Most of the remainder came from organizations with more than 2,000 employees. More than a quarter of respondents were executive management. Twenty percent of respondents identified themselves as IT professionals, 30% as business, and 40% as analytics.

The results show that early adopters are breaking away, and many kinds of cloud-based predictive analytic solutions have potential. Although industries vary in their maturity, the use of cloud-based predictive analytics to improve an organization's focus on customers is particularly powerful. Early adopters look likely to build a sustained competitive advantage.

"What's most impressive? It's the amount of money (millions of dollars) that can be returned to the company's bottom line using good predictive analytics."

—*Survey respondent*

Business Solutions Focus

Most potential buyers of predictive analytics in the cloud are not specifically looking for "cloud" solutions. Years of successful industry adoptions of predictive analytics and growing awareness are resulting in more demand for analytically based solutions. Yet many organizations are not looking for "predictive analytic" solutions either. The vast majority of organizations seek a solution to a specific business challenge. Predictive analytics can help them address the challenges they face. A cloud-based approach can make these solutions faster to deploy, more cost-effective, and more collaborative. Whatever deployment method they adopt, the primary driver is a need for a solution to a business problem.

Organizations realize that technology is not enough, that they also need best practices and industry- or solution-specific implementation. Few solutions are purely software-based; most involve configuration and specialization to work for a specific organization. This requires domain expertise as well as technical know-how. Moreover, embedding predictive analytics often involves significant business change, starting with a willingness to experiment.

This business solution focus goes back to some of the earliest "cloud-based" predictive analytic solutions. Nearly 30 years ago, credit card processors offered hosted and shared applications for fraud detection and credit risk management. A key driver of the adoption of these packages was a desire on the part of banks and credit card issuers to get access to advanced analytic solutions as a packaged offering. This driver remains front and center decades later.

"Tools must be easy for my business teams to use and understand the results; they aren't sophisticated modelers!"

—*Survey respondent*

Five Key Opportunities

The research revealed five common deployment patterns for cloud-based predictive analytics, each offering opportunities for organizations. These five areas include complete solutions, ways to use the cloud to push analytics into existing solutions, and ways to use the cloud to more effectively build predictive analytic models.

Prepackaged Cloud-Based "Decisions as a Service" Solutions

These are cloud-based or software as a service (SaaS) offerings that provide predictive analytics for decision-making as a core feature. Examples include cloud-based applications offering next-best action, offer selection, fraud detection, or instant credit decisions.

They are domain-specific packaged applications that make or enable specific decisions that can be described in business terms. Predictive analytic models are embedded within a solution framework so that the customer receives better decisions, not simply predictions.

For example, a multichannel cross-sell application decides which products to offer customers in different channels, and when. This is based on analytic models that predict how likely it is that the customer in question will buy each product and on rules and policies regarding how and when the products are sold.

These predictive models may be built automatically by software embedded in the solution or built by the solution provider directly. Customers do not have to build their own models, but the models may be built using the customer's own data. However, some of these models are built using data pooled from many organizations, so multiple customers of the solution have the same predictive analytic models. For instance, applications for credit card fraud detection may use scores developed from credit card transactions across multiple card issuers to predict how likely a particular transaction is to be fraudulent.

Predictive Analytics for Software as a Service

These cloud-based solutions inject predictive analytics into other software that is cloud-based or delivered as SaaS. Examples include embedding customer churn predictions in SaaS CRM solutions or delivering risk predictions into cloud-based dashboards.

Many SaaS applications don't include predictive analytics. A cloud-based predictive analytics solution may be the most effective way to embed more-advanced analytics into these operational systems. Predictive analytics or scores are delivered using the cloud to improve the accuracy of decisions already being made by the SaaS application.

For example, a credit risk score could be delivered to a SaaS CRM solution and then used by a customer routing script to route customers with low credit scores to an agent who specializes in helping those with poor credit. The predictive analytic models in question could be developed by the customer, the solution provider, or a third party. They also could be based on pooled data, as discussed in the preceding section. The models could be built automatically using software or built using an existing analytic infrastructure. Regardless, the focus is on making those predictions available to SaaS or cloud-based applications.

Predictive Analytics for Legacy Systems

These cloud-based solutions inject predictive analytics into in-house systems and multichannel environments. Examples include embedding risk scores into a legacy underwriting application or using cloud-based deployment as a bridge to deploy propensity-to-buy models across multiple customer-facing systems.

Most of a typical organization's legacy systems do not use predictive analytics to drive their behavior. In addition, many predictive analytic models are built by organizations and then are not deployed because there is no efficient way to do so. These undeployed models represent lost opportunity. With the pervasiveness of cloud-based solutions and the ease with which applications can be connected to the cloud, a cloud-based predictive analytic deployment approach may significantly increase the effective use of predictive analytic models, especially in legacy applications.

The characteristics of cloud-based services to deliver predictive analytics to on-premises applications are very similar to those embedding predictive analytics in SaaS systems. The target systems may include applications of suppliers and other business partners. For example, a product's predicted target price might need to be distributed to multiple channel partners who each have their own systems. Predictive analytic models with this deployment are more likely to be the organization's own, built in-house or in the cloud.

Modeling with the Data Cloud

This is using cloud-based predictive analytic solutions to respond to the increasing amount of relevant data available in the cloud rather than on-premises. Examples include building predictive analytic models using customer purchase and behavior data stored in a SaaS CRM system, as well as third-party data available from a cloud-based web service.

An increasing number of the data sources that an organization needs to use to build predictive analytic models are available in the cloud. Where previously organizations had on-premises solutions that contained all their customer, sales transaction, human resources, marketing, and web data, now this data is often stored in SaaS and cloud-based solutions. In addition, social media and other unstructured data are often available only through the cloud. The increasingly widespread adoption of big-data technology is driven in part by a need to access and analyze the large volumes of new data available in the cloud. Pooled data supplied by members of a business consortium is also likely to be collected in the cloud.

Modeling with the data cloud pulls all the data available in SaaS applications as well as third-party web services into a cloud-based data management and modeling environment. It pushes predictive analytic modeling to the cloud next to this data so that an organization's whole analytic team can access it, and build models against it, from anywhere.

Elastic Compute Power for Modeling

This is using cloud technology to provide predictive analytics solutions that can scale elastically to meet demand. Examples include assigning extra resources dynamically when optimization or other demanding algorithms are being used to build or run sophisticated predictive analytic models against large datasets.

When companies are building and using predictive analytic models, the amount of computing power needed varies widely during the process. Building predictive analytic models in the cloud offers potentially infinite scaling because clouds (private or public) can deliver elastic computing power. This makes it easy to add and provision new hardware as needed for modeling activities rather than requiring a predefined amount of hardware to be purchased, provisioned, and configured.

For instance, when large datasets must be analyzed or when complex simulations are required to produce predictive analytic models, the team needs a lot more processing power than when they are analyzing results or investigating the data. This scalability is increasingly common in the tools used to build predictive analytic models, but it is by no means pervasive. It may require significant development effort to parallelize and distribute algorithms.

The State of the Market

The market for cloud-based predictive analytic solutions is clearly growing, and early adopters have seen some positive results. Our survey showed a matching increase in confidence, the value of a focus on decision management, and the continuing strength of "traditional" structured data in predictive analytic modeling.

Early Adopters, Competitive Advantage

Survey respondents who have the most experience with predictive analytics are moving more aggressively and with greater confidence. These organizations were

- More likely to have plans to adopt more cloud-based predictive analytic solutions
- Much less likely to have performance or privacy concerns about the solutions
- More likely to embed predictive analytics in operational systems, a driver of positive ROI
- More likely to take advantage of big data from the cloud

Respondents already deploying at least one cloud-based predictive analytics solution are much more likely to adopt solutions going forward. These early adopters contrast with those not yet using cloud-based predictive analytics, who see themselves as much less likely to adopt solutions of any kind. This was true even of packaged solutions, the most preferred option for those who have not yet adopted any solution.

Not only are those already adopting cloud-based predictive analytic solutions getting positive results, but these results make them more likely to accelerate and broaden their adoption of these solutions. Those hesitating about adopting them run the risk that they will be left behind, watching early adopters establish a lead that grows with time.

Decision Management Increases the Value of Analytics

Decision management was clearly an important element for successful analytics adopters, especially as they embedded predictive analytics in operational systems. Survey respondents reporting transformational impact from predictive analytics were much more likely to integrate predictive analytics into operations. As shown in Figure 8.1, the initial impact often comes from occasional use of predictive analytics. But more impact is reported as predictive analytics are used in more operational decision-making.

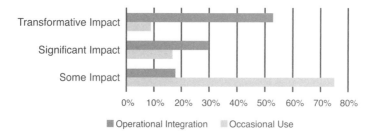

Figure 8.1 The impact of predictive analytics.

Continued Strength of Traditional Data Sources

Survey results showed that structured data from cloud sources was the most important source for building predictive analytic models in the cloud. That was followed by pooled data (structured data from multiple companies pooled for analysis) and structured data uploaded from on-premises solutions to the cloud. Despite all the hype around the unstructured data component of "big data," it seems that structured data still rules in predictive analytics. In addition, those with the most experience in building predictive analytics in the cloud were very positive about the value of both static and batch data. These experienced users were less excited about moving to real-time data than those who lacked experience. Real-time data, it seems, is widely expected to produce better results by those with limited experience. Those who have successfully built and deployed models seem to know that this is not necessarily true.

Taken together, this implies that organizations can get started with predictive analytics and get positive results from using predictive analytic models, even if those models are built only from structured data in a batch environment.

Pros and Cons

Like all things, cloud-based predictive analytic solutions have clear pros and cons. Pros include time to value, pervasiveness, agility, scalability, and data access. Cloud-based predictive analytic solutions have a much faster time to value than alternatives, and the pervasiveness of the cloud is a major factor in this value. Because cloud-based solutions focus on simple, standardized interfaces, they are easy to deploy and adapt. As organizations increase their consumption of predictive analytic models, the value of scalability offered by the cloud will only grow, especially as new sources of data emerge in the cloud.

Against these clear advantages are some cons, such as concerns about privacy and security, regulatory issues, bandwidth for moving data to the cloud, and increased complexity. Keeping the data used in building predictive analytics private and secure is an ongoing challenge, in the cloud or out, and many regulators are uncomfortable with data in the cloud. Even when these challenges are overcome, some organizations find that moving data to the cloud is a challenge due to the fairly narrow "pipes" available at the edge of the Internet. Finally, because cloud-based solutions are still somewhat new and unfamiliar, that creates potential complexity.

Our study found that organizations that have had positive results with cloud-based predictive analytics worry less about data security and privacy, about complexity, and about latency and responsiveness. Familiarity results in a slight decrease in the severity of these concerns. That said, these concerns are particularly strong in industries where the core data required for predictive analytics is regulated data. It is also clear that some of the variation in cloud choices (public, private, or hybrid) is driven by these concerns. Private clouds, for instance, are preferred where the data involved is sensitive or where responsiveness is critical.

Adopting Cloud-Based Predictive Analytics

"There is really no debate anymore on whether to add or not to add analytics to the information technology and business activities within an organization. Instead the debate centers on how to make the best use of the myriad of analytical opportunities that are out there."

—*Jane Griffin, Principal, Deloitte Consulting LLP, and Tom Davenport, IIA Research Director and Senior Advisor, Deloitte Analytics*

The basic value proposition of predictive analytics in the cloud is clear: Organizations can make predictive analytics more scalable, more pervasive, and easier to deploy using cloud technologies. As more organizations seek competitive advantage through analytics, they need the ability to rapidly make analytics pervasive and to tightly integrate analytics into their business strategy and day-to-day operations. For many of the challenges organizations face on their journey toward becoming analytic competitors, cloud-based solutions have much to offer.

Before adopting cloud-based predictive analytic solutions, organizations should understand where they fall on the maturity curve: just getting started with predictive analytics, with some experience but not yet widespread use of predictive analytics, or using predictive analytics regularly and looking for ways to be even more effective.

The different kinds of solutions available under the umbrella of predictive analytics in the cloud enable organizations at every level to adopt cloud-based predictive analytics. They can use cloud-based solutions to jump-start their adoption of predictive analytics, speed and support expansion of use, or refine an already sophisticated approach. The different solutions also enable different parts of an organization to progress differently. More sophisticated or experienced departments can have different adoption strategies than those with no prior predictive analytics experience.

The research and survey results make it clear that organizations should make cloud-based predictive analytics part of both their development approach and deployment architecture. Cloud-based predictive analytics make it easier to adopt new data sources, especially cloud-based big data. The cloud improves the effectiveness of scarce modeling experts by making the power they need available on demand. The pervasiveness of the cloud and the simplicity of its interfaces make it a compelling platform for analytic models, helping to put predictive analytics to work throughout an organization's operational systems, processes, and decisions.

Endnote

1. The survey was conducted in 2011. The research study was sponsored by Clario Analytics, FICO, Opera Solutions, Predixion Software, SAS, Teradata, and Toovio. Full details of the research study are available at http://smartdatacollective. com/predictive-analytics-cloud.

9

Analytical Technology and the Business User

Thomas H. Davenport

It's clear that long-term changes are taking place in the technology environment for business analytics. However, to understand the technology environment of the next five years, it's useful to understand that during the last five—actually, the last 10 or 20—analytics have been a relatively stable technology. In this chapter I'll briefly describe nine different attributes of the past business analytics technology environment, each of which is likely to change in the future. Later in this chapter I'll describe how these attributes will change in the future analytical technology environment.

The past technology environment for business analytics and business intelligence was a relatively monolithic environment, with both quantitative analysts and business users being expected to employ the same tools and data sources. That environment worked relatively well for professional analysts, but the much larger group of business users generally were not served well by it.

Separate but Unequal

The technological environment for business analytics is largely separate from the rest of the application environment for most organizations. It was intentionally separated from the transaction system environment because organizations didn't want to risk problems with transaction systems by directly analyzing their data. Analysis functions were kept separate from transaction functions, and data was kept

123

separate from transaction databases in a warehouse. The two environments were unequal in that companies almost always spent far more on implementing transaction systems than on capabilities to analyze their data.

Staged Data

The preceding discussion of separated transaction systems and analytics suggests that the data for analysis in the current paradigm comes from one source: a data warehouse or mart. This acted as a staging area for access by analytical applications and tools. If you wanted data in your warehouse, you first had to follow an extract, transform, and load (ETL) process to get the data out of your transaction system and into your warehouse or mart. If you wanted to employ data originating in multiple business systems, extensive integration activities typically preceded even the ETL process. If you are working in a big-data environment with massive volumes of data or highly unstructured data, the efforts needed to get your data in a position to be analyzed typically dwarf the efforts to actually analyze the data.

Multipurpose

Since at least the 1970s, analytical capabilities have been multipurpose. Users were provided an extensive toolbox of analytical methods and tools. It was the job of the analyst or decision-maker to decide what tools were appropriate for what analytical context. This, of course, required a high degree of sophistication—one that many analysts and almost all decision-makers lacked. Many data environments for analytics were also multipurpose. The idea behind an enterprise data warehouse is to support a variety of analyses and decisions. Less-popular data marts were intended to support a single type of analysis, or at least a narrow range.

Generally Complex

For both avoidable and unavoidable reasons, analytical technology environments typically are complex. As mentioned, the tool choices typically are quite large, which increases complexity. Serious analytical tools tend to have less-than-ideal user interfaces, although leading vendors have made inroads into solving this problem. Large data warehouses are complex as well. Finally, analytical technology environments will probably always be somewhat difficult to use because analytics themselves are a complex discipline. How many students have difficulty with statistics in school? Despite all the efforts that analytical software providers have made to insulate business users from statistics-driven complexity, an underlying element of quantitative skill is required to succeed with analytics.

Premises- and Product-Based

Analytical tools generally have been based on the customer premises and have been sold primarily as products, rather than as services or solutions. This may contribute to the complexity problem, in that having to worry about memory and storage limitations and other implementation issues are problems for users. Despite the enthusiasm for software as a service (SaaS) and cloud computing, however, this has been one of the relatively less problematic aspects of the analytical environment.

Industry-Generic

Historically, the analytical tools sold to a customer in one industry were the same tools provided to a customer in another. There was little or no tailoring of tools for particular industries. This is despite the fact that each industry has business problems that are best solved with a particular analytical approach. And transaction software (such as ERP) vendors have long customized their products by industry. Although a solution to almost any industry-specific problem can be cobbled together with generic analytical tools, the skills to do this are not widely available. This has begun to change in the past several years, as vendors have offered products specifically designed for some industries, such as money laundering and fraud prevention in banking.

Exclusively Quantitative

Analytics in the past have been almost exclusively quantitative, relying on structured quantitative data and employing algorithms and models to analyze it. This was not a major problem when there were no tools for analyzing other types of data (such as text, voice, and video) and no other approach to supporting decisions (such as business rules). As noted in Chapter 1, even when text and images are being analyzed (as in many big-data contexts), the data about them needs to be converted into structured quantitative data before it can be analyzed.

Business Unit-Driven

Historically, many decisions about the technology to be used for business analytics in organizations were made by managers in charge of particular business units or functions. Their unit had particular decisions to make or problems to solve, so they acquired the software (and often the data storage) to address that particular issue. In effect, they created departmental systems that ran on departmental servers and were maintained by semiprofessional IT people in the business units. This approach ensured that the technology met the specific business need, but it also meant that different departments acquired different analytical technologies, leading to a proliferation of tools and vendors throughout the organization.

Specialized Vendors

Historically, analytics software has been available only through stand-alone, dedicated analytics vendors. Those vendors sold only (or at least primarily) analytics software. One implication of this vendor segregation is the separation of analytics from other software-based activities mentioned earlier. This makes it more difficult to integrate analytical tools and capabilities into transaction systems.

Problems with the Current Model

The current environment worked well for some user classes but not so well for others. Professional analysts generally were well-served in the past environment. It was often a separate world in which an analyst could explore to his or her heart's content. All the data and analytical methods that he or she could ever need were available, and any question could be answered, any decision supported. This was an excellent environment for those with high levels of analytical, technological, and information management skills.

However, for business users, the analytical technology environment has been overly complex. There have been too many tools in the toolbox and too much data in the warehouse. Business users find it difficult to master a broad array of tools, and they don't know how to get the data they need out of the warehouse. The BI industry has spoken for years about "self-service" queries and reporting, and about executives "drilling down" into data, but it simply doesn't happen very often.

Another problem for the current technology environment for business analytics is that the technology is either too close to or too far from the decisions it is supposed to support. In the case of highly departmental applications, the technology does support a specific decision, but it may be difficult to scale or be shared across the company. In the case of highly automated decisions, the analytical tools and the decision are so close as to be one and the same, but developing automated decision engines is difficult. In the multitool, multidata, multipurpose environment described earlier, the technology is too far from the decisions it is designed to support. Software is too difficult for business users to employ, and enterprise data warehouses are too vast.

Because of these problems, there is clearly a need for a new technology environment for business analytics. However, the change will take place in different ways for different user groups. In particular, the technology environment for the business user—the nonprofessional analyst who still needs to create reports and analyses from data—is the one in greatest need of simplification and change.

Changes Emerging in Analytical Technology

This section describes how the analytical technology environment is either already beginning to change, or promises to change in the future, for business users. The most important aspect of the future environment is that it is no longer monolithic. There is not one future environment, but rather three different ones, as shown in Figure 9.1. The BI starburst in the upper left is the multipurpose, multitool environment of the past, which was intended to service both professional analysts and business users. Because the latter was a much larger group, the figure portrays it primarily in that group's camp.

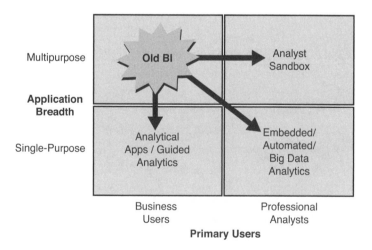

Figure 9.1 The changing analytical technology environment.

Because the multipurpose BI environment didn't serve business users well, future environments won't be in that cell of the matrix. Instead, they'll evolve into three other primary environments:

- The single-purpose environment for business users, which I call *analytical applications* because of their resemblance to apps on iPhones and other smartphones. This environment is simple to use and allows business users to easily find the data and produce the queries and reports they need to make specific decisions. Because of their simplicity and small size, these apps should accelerate the cycle of insights-to-decisions-to-action for many managers and organizations. This is the newest analytical environment. These apps will also guide business users through a decision process; some have called this function *guided analytics*.

- The multipurpose environment for professional analysts, which I'll call the *analyst sandbox*. This environment provides multiple tools and data sources for analysts who can understand them all and effectively choose from among them. It consists of multifunction statistical "packages" such as SAS, SPSS, or R, as well as complex data warehouses with multiple types of data. It is similar to the "old BI" environment, except that there is no longer an assumption that it serves business users, so it doesn't have to be simplified. Its primary purpose can be the creation of advanced analytics, rather than standard or ad hoc reports. In many organizations this environment already exists (although it could always be improved), so it will undergo the least change of the three.

- The single-purpose environment for professional analysts, which I'll call *embedded analytics*. The primary reason for involving professional analysts in single-purpose applications is to achieve scale and real-time delivery. This environment also includes automated decision applications, which almost always need to be developed by analytical professionals. It is also the province of big-data applications requiring professional data science skills. Relatively few such embedded analytics environments exist today, but when they do, they require the technological and analytical skills of professional analysts. They are growing rapidly in the big-data context.

Creating the Analytical Apps of the Future

In contrast to the analytical environment of the past, the next set of attributes characterize the emerging environment for analytical technology as it relates to business users.

Single-Purpose, Industry-Specific, and Simple

Going forward, for relatively simple analytical applications for business users requiring human exploration and interpretation (that is, nonembedded analytics), multipurpose analytical packages are not appropriate. Instead, we'll see analytical "apps," or single-purpose tools that are linked to a particular type of decision. If you need to do a sales forecast, the app will do that and nothing more.

Moreover, I believe that these tools will be tied closely to a particular industry. The sales forecasting tool will be designed to forecast retail sales or discrete manufacturing sales. If you want to do shipment load optimization in a transportation firm, there will be an app for that. The industry-specific apps will know what data is typically employed in an industry and will be able to link to that data easily with only a modicum of system integration work. The combination of decision types and industries will eventually yield thousands of discrete apps.

Like iPhone apps, these tools will be relatively simple to use and will be "guided." They will have intuitive, touch-based interfaces. They will guide users through the process of analyzing the data and even making the resulting decision. Not only will they do the needed calculations on the data, but they also will steer the user through the process of ensuring that the data are well-suited to it, interpreting the results, and making a decision based on the data. They should provide a faster and better return on information in many business analytics domains.

These analytical apps may be developed by software vendors, consultants and integrators, or internal developers (typically IT professionals and professional analysts) within organizations. For example, several "analytic applications" are now available from SAP, although the company envisions that they will eventually be created by a broad ecosystem. Many of the applications thus far have been "co-created" with particular customers. The following are some early applications and their intended industries:

- Health care: quality management
- Health care: nursing productivity
- Telecommunications: customer management and retention
- Banking: enterprise risk and reporting
- Government: planning and consolidation
- Defense: readiness assessment

If this model takes off, there will ultimately be thousands of these applications, some industry-specific and some horizontal. Some will be developed by vendors and some by companies that are users of analytics.

For an example within a company, professional analysts in the Commercial Analytics groups at Merck have developed an analytical app for determining whether a vacancy in the sales force should be filled. The tool accesses the data necessary to perform the analysis and leads the business user—normally a regional sales manager— through the decision process. Also in the pharmaceutical industry, a consultant makes available single-purpose, industry-specific tools for sales forecasting and promotion analysis. Perhaps at some point there will be an "app exchange" for companies to sell or exchange analytical apps that are not deemed to provide competitive advantage.

Service- and Solution-Based

It would be consistent with the analytical apps environment to have application services delivered as services, rather than as premises-based products. That's a simpler approach to providing such apps, and business users wouldn't have to worry about new versions and updates. Service-based applications would also facilitate the use of analytics on mobile devices for industry and process contexts that require them. Not surprisingly, many vendors are beginning to offer analytics as a service, and I expect this trend to continue and accelerate—particularly for analytical apps environments. Deloitte, for example, offers a Managed Analytics service with a variety of single-function analytical applications, including the following:

- Transportation analysis
- Aftermarket services revenue growth
- Transportation contract compliance
- Services operations and warranty analysis

Solutions consisting of bundled products and professional services may not be as necessary in the future as they are today because apps will be simpler for business users to use. However, it is possible that services will still be necessary to configure apps and ensure that they are drawing on the correct data sources. For this reason, it's reasonable to expect some degree of solutions orientation on the part of major vendors.

Centrally Coordinated

It seems ironic that in a shift to analytical apps for business users, there will be more coordination by a central IT function. After all, there is little or no central coordination for iPhone apps. However, even with analytical apps, there will be a need for some central coordination, although business users will probably initiate their use. They will need to be developed and integrated, and some of that work will be done by internal IT organizations. They will also require data, and IT and data management professionals will need to help provide it. And for apps that are popular across enterprises, vendors may well provide site-license pricing that would require central coordination and distribution. Finally, to avoid the "multiple versions of the truth" problem, these experts need to ensure that different analytical applications don't overlap and that similar applications use similar data.

Of course, for embedded analytics and analytical sandboxes, IT organizations typically have played important roles in the past, and they will continue to do so. In big-data environments, technology-oriented professionals will be even more important than in the past.

Integrated Vendors

For both analytical apps and embedded analytics applications, separate analytics vendors are becoming part of larger integrated firms offering transaction processing software and services. Of course, this transformation is already largely complete: Large software and hardware providers have already acquired most of the freestanding analytical and business intelligence software vendors. These large, integrated vendors are beginning to introduce offerings that integrate analytical capabilities with other software tools. Examples of this integration include the following:

- Creating small analytical apps that link to particular modules of transaction software. An example is a trade promotion analysis application linked to the trade promotion transaction system for a retail ERP system.

- Embedding analytics and algorithms into transaction software. An example is introducing an automatically calculated *customer lifetime value* analysis into the order management function of an ERP system.

- Implementing *in-database processing* of calculations for more rapid processing of data-intensive analytics. (Independent analytics vendors are pursuing this same approach through partnerships and alliances.)

- Inclusion of reporting—if not advanced analytics—capabilities in the *in-memory* versions of transaction software, which offer rapid response and click-based report design.

- Incorporation of data warehouse, data mart, and on-demand data assembly by traditional database and storage vendors.

The remaining independent analytics vendors will attempt to match this integration by focusing primarily on the analytical sandbox and by increased emphasis on partnerships and alliances for embedded analytics. Large services and systems integration vendors are also incorporating analytics into their practices in a substantial way. These firms also focus heavily on transactional and other enterprise software capabilities and are likely to be active in integrating analytical functions into those environments.

Summary

These changes in the technology environment for business user-centric analytics are already happening and will become more widely distributed over time. Some organizations may need to emphasize one of the future environments more than others. Those with primarily reporting needs will probably emphasize analytical apps, and firms needing a lot of advanced analytics may emphasize the analytical sandbox. Firms with a strong process and transaction orientation may emphasize the embedded analytics environment. Although analytical apps may represent the bulk of business analytics activity because of the large size of the user base, most large organizations will probably need elements of all three environments to support their key decisions with data and analysis. Particularly for business user analytics, we are likely to see more change in the next few years of analytical technology than we have seen in the last few decades. This change is long overdue. It promises a much closer and more effective link between information and decision-making than ever before.

10

Linking Decisions and Analytics for Organizational Performance[1]

Thomas H. Davenport

If the goal of better information—and better analysis of it—is ultimately better decisions and actions taken based on them, organizations must have a strong focus on decisions and their linkage to information. Businesses need to address how decisions are made and executed, how they can be improved, and how information is used to support them. And they must look at all types of decisions. This includes strategic planning decisions made by senior management to everyday operational decisions made by employees on the front line, or automated by back-end systems.

Improving decision processes has obvious benefits. Many organizations suffer from poor decision processes and outcomes. There is a growing body of knowledge on optimal decision processes and decision biases to avoid,[2] but it is often ignored or misapplied within organizations. Information and analytics that are available to inform decisions aren't used, or information is captured and managed that is unsuitable for decision purposes. Information is valued and analyzed differently across different contexts.[3] Decisions frequently take too long to make,[4] and organizations lack clarity on who should make them.[5] In assessing decision processes, we hardly know the extent of the problem and the potential benefits, for few organizations identify, assign clear responsibility for, or track the results of their key decisions.

A Study of Decisions and Analytics

In this chapter I describe a study of attempts by organizations to improve decision-making through the use of information and analytics, among other interventions. Using telephone interviews in the second half of 2008, I spoke with 32 managers in 27 organizations about specific initiatives their organizations had undertaken to improve decisions or decision processes. In each interview I asked about why the initiative had been undertaken, how the decision process varied before and after the intervention, and what steps were taken to provide the decision process and decision-makers with better or more trusted information and analysis. The research sites were selected based on press accounts of decision-oriented business intelligence applications or references from business intelligence vendor personnel. Thus they were more likely to use analytics than might be expected from a random sample.

My intent was to understand how information and analytics are being applied to improve decision-making in a broad range of contexts. The following is a list of the decision types and organizational contexts. Most of the decisions listed are made frequently and involve core business processes of the organization. I sought out such core processes because it seemed that they would be the most likely to be the subject of initiatives to supply information and analytics for decisions.

Types of Decisions Studied:

- Supply chain and financial decisions in an electronics distributor
- Credit and risk decisions in a money center bank
- Marketing and performance management decisions in a fast food restaurant chain
- Performance management and supply chain decisions in a vehicle manufacturer
- Merchandising and loyalty decisions in a retail department store chain
- New-product development decisions in a testing and research organization
- Credit and risk decisions in a consumer finance company

- Energy project credit decisions in an energy finance company
- Real estate finance decisions in a commercial real estate financing company
- Sales decisions in an IT product and service firm
- Retail financial services decisions in a banking and insurance firm
- Claims and disease management decisions in a health insurer
- Project estimation decisions in a defense contractor
- Student performance decisions in two different urban school districts
- Pricing decisions in an industrial equipment firm
- Physician drug ordering decisions in an academic medical center
- Critical care decisions in a hospital
- Logistical decisions in a trucking firm
- Pricing decisions in a carpeting manufacturer
- Financial and disease management decisions in a health insurer
- Organ donation decisions in an organ-sharing network
- Student performance decisions in a public university
- Small business insurance underwriting and delivery in a major insurance firm
- Oil drilling decisions in a midsize integrated oil company
- New greeting card decisions at a greeting card company
- Automobile financing decisions in a sales and financing company

Although most of the managers interviewed were comfortable talking about attempts to bring about better decisions, the topic was not yet top of mind in most companies. It was clear in the discussions that most firms had not focused consciously on better decisions as an area for business improvement. Some had not initially viewed their efforts as decision-oriented; this was true, for example, at a testing and research firm, which was attempting to improve its new-product development processes. The manager interviewed stated, however, that the key issue in the process was making decisions about which products to develop.

There were some exceptions, however, to the "invisibility" of decisions. Two large banks, for example, had created *decision management* groups that focused on analytical and quantitative decision processes. One major consumer products firm had renamed its IT organization Information and Decision Solutions. The organization contained substantial numbers of analysts who assisted decision-makers with analytics and fact-based decision processes. While these organizations are moving toward a stronger focus on decision-making, most do not seem to have broad agendas in place for connecting information and decisions in general. But they may have particular decision emphases such as greater use of analytics or automated decisions.

Linking Decisions and Analytics

How do organizations ensure that decisions are made on the basis of the best possible information and analytics? In the research interviews, I discovered at least three different levels of relationship between analytics and decision-making (see Figure 10.1), each of which were present in the organizations interviewed for this study. The primary variable describing differences between the levels is the degree of structure in the decision, which has appeared frequently in the business intelligence and decision support literature.[6]

Loosely Coupled Analytics and Decisions

Perhaps the most common approach to linking analytics and decision-making is to loosely couple the two. That is, organizations often make information broadly accessible to analysts and decision-makers for application to decisions, along with tools to analyze and display the information. The information usually involves a particular business domain—finance, marketing, sales, or overall performance management, for example. However, it is intended to inform a range of possible decisions. The actual use of the information and analytics for any particular decision is voluntary and based on individual initiative. There is no monitoring of what information or analyses are used for which decisions, either before or after decisions are made.

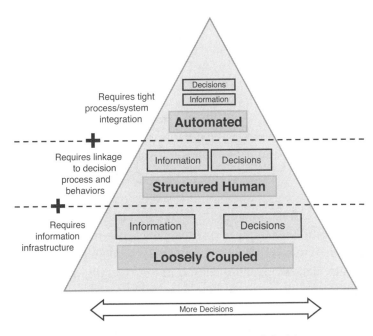

Figure 10.1 Three approaches to linking information and decisions.

This loosely coupled approach would characterize most organizations' approaches to business intelligence, or what was previously called *decision support*. Data suitable for analysis and decision-making is extracted from transaction systems and is made available in a data warehouse or mart. Standard reports are produced, perhaps in easier-to-understand "scorecard" or "dashboard" formats. The analytics employed typically are reporting or descriptive analytics.

The appeal of this approach is that providers of information—an IT organization, for example—can supply the information without regard to difficult and sensitive issues such as managerial psychology, organizational politics, and decision rights. In such decision environments, more structure or automation may be inappropriate or unnecessary. In this model it is not the task of the information provider (or anyone else) to ensure that the decision is informed by the information or is made well. Also appealing is that a single information infrastructure can support a variety of decisions, which is productive and efficient for information providers.

However, although it does not directly address managerial decision processes, this loosely coupled approach still presents many challenges. To provide information and analysis suitable for decision-making, information usually must be integrated from multiple source systems and be of high quality. Organizations also struggle with developing "a single version of the truth" so that information for decisions is consistent across the organization. It is easy for multiple versions of reports and data entities to proliferate across large, complex organizations.

I found several examples of this loosely coupled approach in the study, and others are common throughout the business intelligence literature.[7] For example, a regional health insurer created a Financial Data Mart to support a variety of financial decisions. The data mart was supplied with high-quality data on operations, product utilization trends, and financial results across the organization. Considerable effort was expended to ensure "a single version of the truth." Training was provided on how to use the system and how to access commonly used reports and data cubes. The IT organization was under the impression that the primary users were much more able to create and apply reports that informed their decisions. Of course, because the specific decisions to be made from the data mart and related analyses were not directly linked, the value to improvements in decision-making remains impossible to calculate.

Other examples of this sort of decision/analytics relationship in the study included a student performance analysis and reporting system in an urban school district, and a somewhat broader business intelligence system at a large university. Both were focused on better understanding student performance; the university's system also addressed research grants, financial management, and human resources. Both were viewed as initially successful by the managers interviewed, and they required similar types of effort and investment as that of the health insurer. The urban school district experienced a decline in usage after the superintendent, the system's primary advocate, left the district. The university's most effective users were in a school where the dean was a strong advocate and user of the system.

As with the university and the school district, making these loosely coupled decision environments work requires much more than simply making analytics available. Firms that had successfully improved decision-making described such approaches as a strong alignment between IT organizations and business units, approaches to developing the users' abilities, and clarity on the business objectives of data warehouses and marts.

Structured Human Decision Environments

Some organizations interviewed had a narrower focus on particular decisions but tried to create an overall decision-making environment that went beyond just establishing an information infrastructure and providing some descriptive analytics capabilities. In this approach, the decision at hand is still made entirely by human managers or professionals. But specific efforts have been made to improve targeted decision processes or contexts by determining the specific information, analytics, and other process resources needed to make better decisions faster.

The advantage of this approach is that these additional efforts created a stronger linkage between the analytics and the relevant decisions, making this approach more likely to be used effectively. The challenges of this approach relative to the loosely coupled one are its narrower focus on particular decisions and the additional effort needed to create the decision environment. If the decision is an important one for organizational success, however, it may be worth the additional effort.

The type of additional support for decision-making varied widely across different examples in the study. In some cases analytical tools and capabilities provided the additional decision support. This was true of pricing decisions at an industrial equipment firm, marketing and performance management decisions in a fast food restaurant chain, and merchandising and loyalty decisions at a retail department store chain. In the industrial equipment pricing example, salespeople were provided with analysis yielding a target price, a floor price, and a ceiling price, based on analysis of previous sales and segmentation of the relative differentiation of the product being sold. At the fast food restaurant, randomized testing analyses were used to support new-product marketing decisions, and econometric models explained which factors drove changes in weekly sales results. At the retail department store chain, predictive models of sales for particular brands were used to order merchandise for stores and regions.

However, in all three examples, analytics were not the only approach to improving the decision environment. There were also investments in establishing accurate, trusted information, along with a focus on organizational and behavioral techniques being employed. At the industrial equipment manufacturer, the company also felt the need to create new divisional pricing manager roles to ensure that salespeople understood the new pricing approaches and adopted them successfully. At the fast food restaurant, the Chief Information Officer employed principles from cognitive science research to maximize the likelihood that executives would notice and understand key information. At the retail department store chain, information providers worked closely with early adopters of the new decision approach to identify ways to spread the use of the approach to less analytically oriented merchandisers. And in all three cases, an information infrastructure was put in place with a particular focus on delivering the right information and analytics needed to support improved decision-making.

A second decision environment at a different urban school district provides a clear example of the difference between loosely coupled and structured human decision environments. At the first district with a loosely coupled analytics and decision environment, the district supplied a data warehouse and business intelligence tools and some training opportunities. The principals and teachers were expected to use the system on their own. At the second school district, the same types of tools were supplied. However, the district also created an *inquiry team* in each school (some other school districts call these *data teams*). Each inquiry team included three to six personnel—primarily teachers, but also the principal. One team member was designated as an expert on the data and the tool set. The teams' goal was to help school personnel define decisions and use the data and tools to address them. District personnel report a higher degree of use and value for the system and data than in the first district that did not employ an equivalent to inquiry teams.

In other cases, organizations employed tools to provide additional structure around the decision process. At an energy finance company, an analyst interviewed senior executives to understand the factors they used in making financing decisions[8] and developed a model of the factors they employed using conjoint analysis. (This is an analytical technique usually employed to understand customer preferences in marketing.) Although senior executives still actually make the decisions, the model has been helpful to less-experienced employees in preparing their financing proposals. Research has shown that decisions made using the factors uncovered in the analysis are substantially more successful than those made with unaided experience and intuition.

At a truck manufacturer, decisions about performance management, supply chain, and other operational issues were incorporated into a broader context. The company had adopted the A3 problem-solving approach as used successfully by Toyota.[9] The approach structures a set of problem resolution and action steps on two sheets of paper (A3 size in Japan). The approach ensures that analytics and decisions result in improved business performance. A greeting card company used considerable market research-based information, and a decision-structuring framework involving customer value, to assess whether a new line of lower-cost greeting cards provided sufficient value to customers. The framework represents customer value as a combination of five factors: equity, experience, energy, product, and money.

Technology also provides support for these structured human decisions. Scorecards such as the *balanced scorecard*[10] and specialized information displays provide just the information needed by decision-makers and no other. Recommendation systems based on algorithms or rules provide a recommended decision. But with these types of decisions they usually can be overridden by human decision-makers—as they were by physicians in an online physician ordering system in an academic medical center.[11]

Given the breadth of the actions and tools that organizations adopt to better connect analytics and decisions and the challenges of addressing managerial behavior, this approach can't be adopted for all decisions. The decisions selected for this sort of intervention must be particularly critical to organizational success. That is, they should involve strategic issues or important everyday decisions that drive business performance. With such interventions, however, the link between analytics and decision-making may be much tighter on average.

Automated Decisions

The closest linkages between analytics and decisions usually come when decisions are made by computer. When it is critical for information and analysis to be applied to a decision in a structured, formulaic fashion, the answer is often to employ automated decision systems.[12] Although artificial intelligence and expert systems garnered the majority of press and visibility two decades ago,[13] many firms have quietly implemented more straightforward automated decision-making in a variety of business domains. To optimize operational decision-making, companies have embedded decision rules and algorithms into key business processes. In doing so, many have achieved greater speed and decision accuracy and better customer service. Although human experts design the system in the first place, with automated decisions they are not the primary decision-makers—they usually come into play only in handling exceptions.

Automated decision-making systems are not a new idea—they first took hold, for example, in *yield management* systems in airlines that made automated pricing decisions in the early 1980s.[14] But the applications for the idea are expanding significantly. After yield management, automated decision-making became pervasive in the financial services industry and is still most common there. In investment banking, these systems are behind the rise of program trading of equities, currencies, and other financial assets. For most consumers, the primary impact of automated decision-making is in the realm of credit approval. Credit scores are used to extend or deny credit to individuals applying for mortgages, credit cards, and other forms of debt. Although credit scoring has been criticized for being overly simplistic, it has certainly made the process more rapid and efficient. There is no longer any doubt that credit score analysis is being applied to decisions that it can inform.

In this study, the automated decision activities were at two large banks; a large, privately held automobile sales and financing firm; and a large property and casualty insurance firm. All four organizations had institutionalized the process of developing and using automated decision systems. The insurance firm had begun using the approach on individual-level underwriting decisions and had extended it to more complex small-business policies. The company also built a special portal for its agents to use in entering data from the system and receiving results. The banks with automated decisions were focused primarily on automated credit and lending decisions. The large automobile leasing and financing firm was re-engineering several of its business processes for automobile financing and using automated decisions to improve the efficiency and effectiveness of recurring financing decisions.

Again, in all four cases, significant investments were made in the underlying information infrastructure. As decisions become automated, it becomes increasingly important to ensure that the information used is complete and accurate because no human is involved in fact checking.

Of course, the development of automated decision systems is time-consuming and expensive. Firms must be selective in deciding which decisions to automate. The decision process must be sufficiently structured and reducible to rules or algorithms, and a complete and direct linkage to all the information needed must be created. Also, decision rules or algorithms should be reviewed frequently to ensure that they continue to produce the right decision outcomes. The automobile leasing and financing firm has a clear set of criteria to identify the processes that are most likely to benefit from automated decisions. The firm is committed to reviewing them frequently for needed revisions. The firm also integrates multiple information technologies to support the re-engineered processes, including a work flow system for coordinating process flow and a rules engine to store and execute business rules. Despite these challenges, automated decision-making provides the closest possible link between decisions and analytics. For this reason it is likely that this process will continue to grow in popularity and effectiveness.

A Process for Connecting Decisions and Information

Given these three options for relating decisions to the information and analyses that inform them, organizations can follow a process for establishing and maintaining the connection. The process may vary somewhat with the particular decision/analytics linkage that the organization follows. Although no organization specifically followed each of these steps in this order, a logical process can be inferred from the organizations interviewed.

Step 1: Strategic Focus on Key Decisions

Because connecting analytics and decision-making often requires a major investment of resources, it's important to ensure that any decision selected for intervention is actually important to the organization's strategy and performance. Therefore, a reasonable first step is for an organization's executives to discuss the strategy and determine what decisions are important to its successful execution. It may be unnecessary to rank the most important decisions, but no organization should waste time and energy on decisions that don't matter. And at least in retrospect, the choice of decisions for intervention often seemed obvious in the examples surveyed.

For example, a European financial services company with major business units in life insurance and banking concluded that it needed to become closer to its customers and offer them a more integrated range of financial services. Its management team decided that decisions about which products to offer which customers were critical to its strategy. After identifying the decision, the company embarked upon a series of efforts to pull together the information environment and analyses that would make an integrated view of customers possible. Better decision-making by customers was also a goal, in that the new online environment would make it possible for them to see all their holdings in one place.

The academic medical center discovered in the 1990s that it had unacceptably high levels of medical errors. The organization's leaders decided that a key decision process was that in which physicians decided which drugs, tests, treatments, and referrals to administer to patients. This process, and information systems that address it, is known in the health care industry as *physician order entry*. The importance of the decision to the institution's primary mission of better patient care is illustrated by the successful result of the order entry intervention: a 55% reduction in "adverse drug events."[15]

Organizations that do not address this strategic step first in their attempts to provide information for decision-making face a key risk. They may end up building information environments that don't help decision processes in business-critical areas. They may be unable to determine whether their efforts were worth the investment of money and time. Still, many organizations, including some in this study, embarked upon substantial information provision projects without any strategic clarity about what particular decisions they support.

Step 2: Information and Analytics Provision

Given an important decision that's key to an organization's strategy, organizations must begin to provide information for it and analytics that will support it. In loosely coupled relationships between decisions and analytics, this is appropriately the second step in the process. If the analytics and the decision are more closely coupled (in structured human decision processes or automated decisions), it may be more appropriate to first undertake Step 3, involving decision design (described next). The order in which information provision and decision design take place also varies by the amount of time it's estimated to take to make information and analytics available to the decision. The provision of information may lead to the development of a data warehouse, a more focused data mart, or a specific analytical application. Either way, the accuracy and completeness of information has a direct impact on the ease and effectiveness of the following steps.

The information and analytics provision step might begin by asking a series of natural questions about the decision:

• What information is required to support the decision?
• How accurate does the information need to be?

- What's the most efficient process for collecting, generating, and supplying the information?
- How should it be transformed analytically?
- In what time frame does the information need to be supplied?

For example, a large national health insurer concluded that its most important decisions were in the areas of claims and such specific activities as claims adjudication, disease management, and claims payment. To address these decisions, the firm's managers concluded that it needed to take a bottom-up look at claims information—how the information is gathered and stored around the company. It is constructing a large enterprise warehouse of claims information. It also is developing what it calls *data communities*—a series of focused data marts dealing with specific business problems related to claims. The relevant departments are also generating the analytical models to support decisions in these areas.

The challenge of the information and analytics provision step—particularly if it is undertaken before decision design—is to keep in mind the specific decisions the information is to inform. It is all too easy to become wrapped up in information management and analytics issues and to lose sight of the decisions involved. Organizations need to make sure they have a business intelligence agenda that is being driven by their business objectives.

Step 3: Decision Design

In this step, the key aspects of the context for the decision being made are designed, or at least evolve in a preferred direction. Important considerations in the design process include identifying the roles that different individuals will play in the decision, the level of structure for the decision, the ability of human decision-makers to process the relevant information and analytics, and the roles of humans versus computers in the decision process.

In the study of 27 decisions, I found a few organizations in which decision processes were explicitly designed. The energy finance company, where the factors driving executive decisions were explicitly modeled and communicated to decision-makers, is one example of a consciously designed decision process. The academic medical center's physician order entry system is another. An auto leasing and financing firm is redesigning many automobile financing processes and is simultaneously addressing the key decisions made in those processes.

More frequently, however, the decision context had simply evolved over time with multiple interventions. For example, at a midsize oil company, the decision involving in which areas to drill for new oil had been the subject of several incremental improvements over time intended to bring greater structure and effectiveness to the decision. The company had invested in a formal Prospect Evaluation Sheet that recorded the story and history of how the lead progressed to its current prospect level. The company had also depicted the exploration decision-making process in a visual analytics format, which greatly enhanced the ability of participants to understand their roles, responsibilities, and interactions throughout the process. Still, despite the company's efforts to better structure the decision and a massive amount of seismic and geological information, the decision process remained more iterative and subjective than some managers would have preferred, and less analytical than the process some other companies employed.

In automated decision processes, organizations must explicitly design not only the rules and/or algorithms that will be embedded in the automated decision system, but also the performance objectives for the process and the role for human experts in designing and operating the system. In the property and casualty insurance underwriting decision process, the company designed the new process to optimize the cost, time, quality, and consistency of policy underwriting, as well as measures of how long it takes to add or change a rule and modify the underwriting criteria. The company followed a rule of thumb for utilizing underwriters to keep the best performers away from routine underwriting. Underwriters should instead do *portfolio management*—looking across all the rules, monitoring performance, and looking for new business areas. The company also specified the conditions under which human underwriters would become involved in handling exceptions, such as those involving high dollar amounts or missing data.

Step 4: Decision Execution

The final step in connecting information, analytics, and decisions might be to operate and manage the decision process over time and to ensure that decision-makers use information and analytics to make better decisions. This step almost certainly involves training users on the available data, on the use of systems to access the data, and perhaps on the factors to consider in decision-making. The regional health insurer, for example, spent considerable resources designing a training program for financially focused users of the business intelligence system and then redesigned the training later to address changes in the business and the available data.

Those who are responsible for ensuring effective use of the information and analytics in decision processes may also want to enlist influential executives as users. As suggested earlier, in the urban school district, the frequent and aggressive use of the system by the superintendent led principals and teachers to make more use of it as well. At the Australian university, the school that used the business intelligence system most effectively had an influential user in the dean of the school.

Organizations will also need to modify and improve their decision processes and analytics over time. At the academic medical center, the physicians can override system recommendations that they disagree with. The institution monitors which treatment decisions are frequently overridden to determine whether they are faulty or unnecessary. The medical center also employs an online discussion system to allow expert physicians to discuss and decide on new treatments to be added to the order entry system over time.[16]

Looking Ahead in Decision Management

Although it is a long-term objective, we are still in the early stages of improving decision-making and making better use of information and analytics in decision processes. As organizations move in this direction, we will undoubtedly learn about new approaches to linking information and analytics to decisions and to improving the broader context for decision-making. We will also probably see new information technologies that attempt to structure and improve decision processes. Even though we now have many of the technological components for better decisions—including data warehouses, business intelligence tools, analytical methods, work flow systems, decision rule engines, and so forth—these components are not yet well-integrated, and organizations are unsure about how they fit together. Perhaps in the future we will have decision management systems that incorporate all these capabilities as well as others. Systems have been used to help select a decision approach in the past, but only in limited contexts.[17]

The primary obstacle to decision improvement efforts is likely to be traditional understandings of management responsibility for decision-making. If organizations view decisions as an individual managerial prerogative—not subject to review or improvement—they are likely to make little progress in making better decisions. Many firms have implicitly treated decision-making in this fashion, and hence they will have difficulty with interventions intended to improve decision-making performance.

Decision-making has always been viewed as one of the most important activities of everyone in an organization, from executives and managers to front- and back-office employees handling everyday customer interactions and transactions. It is difficult to overestimate the value of improving decision-making. Decisions affect every aspect of organizational performance, in both strategic and tactical domains. Organizations have too much at stake to continue with the poor decision processes of the past. It seems timely for them to address better decision-making as one of the last—and most important—frontiers of business performance improvement.

Endnotes

1. This chapter is derived from an IIA research brief, a white paper sponsored by IBM, and an article, "Business Intelligence and Organizational Decisions. *International Journal of Business Intelligence Research* (*IJBIR*), 1(1), 1–12, 2010.

2. Hammond, J., Keeney, R., and Raiffa, H., 1998. "The Hidden Traps in Decision Making," *Harvard Business Review*, September.

3. Tversky, A., and Kahneman, D., 1974. "Judgment under uncertainty: Heuristics and biases," *Science*, *185(4157)*, 1124–1131.

4. Eisenhardt, K. and Brown, S., 1998. "Time Pacing: Competing in Markets That Won't Stand Still," *Harvard Business Review*, March.

5. Rogers, P. and Blenko, M., 2006. "Who Has the D? How Clear Decision Roles Enhance Organizational Performance," *Harvard Business Review*, January.

6. See, for example, Simon, H.A., 1960. *The New Science of Management Decision*. New York: Harper & Row.

7. See, for example, Howson, C., 2007. *Successful Business Intelligence*. McGraw-Hill.

8. Venditti, P., Donald Peterson, D., and, Siegel, M., 2007. "Evaluating Financial Deals Using a Holistic Decision Modeling Approach," paper presented to Sawtooth Software conference, Santa Rosa, CA, October 17.

9. Dennis, P., 2006. *Getting the Right Things Done: A Leader's Guide to Planning and Execution*, Lean Enterprise Institute.

10. Norton, D. and Kaplan, R., 1993. "Putting the Balanced Scorecard to Work," *Harvard Business Review*, September.

11. Davenport, T.H. and Glaser, J., 2002. "Just-In-Time Delivery Comes to Knowledge Management," *Harvard Business Review*, July.

12. See, for example, Taylor, J. and Raden, N., 2007. *Smart Enough Systems: How to Deliver Competitive Advantage by Automating Hidden Decisions*. Prentice-Hall.

13. See, for example, Kurzweil, R., 1990. *Age of Intelligent Machines*. MIT Press.

14. Ingold, A., McMahon-Beattie, U., and Yeoman, I., 2001. *Yield Management*. New York: Continuum.

15. Bates, D.W. et al, 1998. "Effect of Computerized Physician Order Entry and a Team Intervention on Prevention of Serious Medication Errors," *Journal of the American Medical Association* 280, Oct. 21, 1311–1316.

16. Hongsermeier, T. and Davenport, T.H., 2007. "Collaborative Treatment: Partners HealthCare," *Inside Knowledge*, December.

17. Vroom, V., 2003. "Educating Managers for Decision-Making and Leadership," *Management Decision, 41(10)*, 968–978.

Part IV
The Human Side of Analytics

11

Organizing Analysts

Robert F. Morison and Thomas H. Davenport

One of the most common questions we hear when discussing organizations' analytical efforts is "How should we best organize our analysts?" It's a common question arising from a common situation: Analysts and analytics projects are scattered across the organization. That's how companies get started with analytics—here and there as pockets of interest arise. However, when an organization starts to get serious about analytics, it has to adopt an enterprise perspective to develop analysts effectively and deploy them where they create the greatest business value. Those pockets of analytics need to be coordinated, consolidated, or centralized.

Why Organization Matters

The trend is clearly toward centralization of analysts, and that makes sense for several reasons. If a company wants to differentiate itself in the marketplace through its analytical capabilities, it doesn't make sense to manage analytics locally. Skilled and experienced analysts are a scarce and high-demand resource. A central agency can deploy them on the most important projects, including cross-functional and enterprise-wide projects that may otherwise be difficult to staff. Centralization also facilitates analyst development because people have more opportunity to connect with and learn from one another. In addition, a central group with a decent population helps with recruiting analysts by demonstrating the organization's commitment to analytics and providing new hires with a community. Finally, research by Accenture[1] shows that analysts in centralized and

157

well-coordinated structures are more engaged and more likely to stay around than their decentralized counterparts.

The second most common situation among organizations we work with is a significant analytics presence in one or two business functions, plus small pockets of analytics across the rest of the organization. The lead functions vary by industry—product development and trading in financial services, engineering and supply chain in manufacturing, marketing in consumer businesses. The challenge is to simultaneously connect the pockets of analytics and spread the wealth of expertise resident in the advanced units. In these cases, full centralization could be unnecessarily disruptive, so the organization needs other mechanisms to coordinate the analyst talent supply.

In the book *Analytics at Work*, we (along with Jeanne Harris) discuss five common organizational models.[2] They're a useful place to start, but organizing your analysts isn't as simple as just picking one. There are different organizational circumstances, many variables in play, and many variations on the theme. This chapter decomposes the organizational models for analysts and provides tools for developing and tuning your own model.

General Goals of Organizational Structure

Let's start with the basics. In addition to their role in employee administration, organizational structures serve two fundamental purposes:

- **Deploying** people on the important and value-adding work of the enterprise. This is about doing today's work and maximizing people's contribution.
- **Developing** people so that they will have the skills and experience for tomorrow's work. This is about maintaining the organization's capability and "health" and maximizing people's individual and collective potential.

These two goals are interrelated because the most important learning and development occur on the job. But they are in opposition whenever there's a choice between deploying someone to employ proven skills on an important project and giving the person a new role or "stretch" assignment. Classic hierarchical organizational structures tend to err on the side of keeping people in their "boxes." Yet analysts will not stay with an organization long unless they have ample variety in their jobs and opportunity to learn.

Organizational design boils down to two big questions:

- What's the best way to *group* people to begin with for purposes of both deployment and development?
- What are the necessary and best ways to *coordinate* across groups? No basic grouping will be perfect in terms of both deployment and development of all staff.

Goals of a Particular Analytics Organization

When debating alternative organizational structures for analytical groups, it's important to keep in mind the overriding goals for the organization. Typically, the goals of analytical groups and their leadership within companies include the following:

- Supporting business decision-makers with analytical capabilities
- Providing leadership and a "critical mass" home for analytical people and the ability to easily share ideas and collaborate on projects across analysts
- Fostering visibility for analytics throughout the organization and ease in finding help with analytical problems and decisions
- Creating standardized methodological approaches, tools, and processes
- Researching and adopting new analytical practices
- Reducing the cost to deliver analytical outcomes
- Building and monitoring analytical capabilities and expertise

Different priorities for these goals may lead to different organizational models. For example, the goal of supporting business decision-makers with analytics may best be served by locating analysts directly in business units and functions that those decision-makers lead. However, such decentralization may work against the goal of helping analysts easily share ideas and collaborate.

No set of organizational structures and processes is perfect or permanent, so organizations must decide what particular goals are most important at any point in their analytical life cycles. For example, if an organization has had a centralized group of analysts for a while and it has become unresponsive to business unit needs, it may be time to establish stronger ties between analysts and specified business units and leaders. A company with highly localized analytics may need to switch, at least for a while, to a more centralized structure.

Basic Models for Organizing Analysts

Figure 11.1 shows the common organizational models described in *Analytics at Work*.

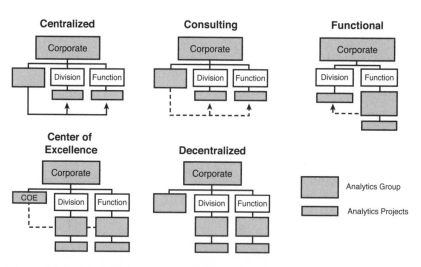

Figure 11.1 Five organizational models.

In a *centralized* model, all analyst groups are part of one corporate organization. Even if located in or primarily assigned to business units or functions, all analysts report to the corporate unit. This obviously makes it easier to deploy analysts on projects with strategic priority, as well as to develop skills and build community. However, especially if the analysts are all housed in the corporate location, it can create distance between analysts and the business. Implementing a centralized model for analytics is easiest where there is successful precedent for operating other functions or managing scarce resources as shared services.

In a *consulting* model, all analysts are part of one central organization, but instead of being deployed from corporate to business unit projects, the business units "hire" analysts for their analytical projects. This model is more market-driven. Especially important here is the analyst/consultants' ability to educate and advise their customers on how to utilize analyst services—in other words, to make the market demand smart. This model can be troublesome if enterprise focus and targeting mechanisms are weak because analysts may end up working on whatever business units choose to pay for (or whatever wheel is squeakiest) rather than what delivers the most business value.

In a *functional* or "best home" model, one major analyst unit reports to the business unit or function that is the primary consumer of analyst services. This analyst unit typically also provides services in a consulting fashion to the rest of the corporation. As already mentioned, many financial services and manufacturing firms have, in effect, a functional model today, with one or two well-established analyst groups in functions such as marketing or risk management. The best home may migrate as analytical applications are completed and the corporation's analytical orientation changes, typically from operations to marketing.

A *center of excellence* model is a somewhat less centralized approach that still incorporates some enterprise-level coordination. In this structure, analysts are based primarily in business functions and units, but their activities are coordinated by a small central group. The CoEs typically are responsible for issues such as training, adoption of analytical tools, and facilitating communication among analysts. The CoE builds a community of analysts and can organize or influence their development and their sharing across units. It is most appropriate for large, diverse businesses that have a variety of analytical needs and issues but that still would benefit from central coordination. This is an analytical version of the Gartner-promoted "business intelligence competency center."

There are many variations on this popular model, depending on the powers of the CoE. Do analysts report to it dotted line? Does it control the staff development agenda and resources? Does it double as a Program Management Office (PMO), with powers to coordinate priorities and resources across business units? Or are the business units solidly in charge of their analysts?

In a *decentralized* model, analyst groups are associated with business units and functions, and there is likely an analytics group or groups for corporate functions, but there is no corporate reporting or consolidating structure. This model makes it difficult to set enterprise priorities and develop and deploy staff effectively through borrowing and rotation of staff. It is most appropriate in a diversified multibusiness corporation where the businesses have little in common. But even then we feel it makes sense to build a cross-business community of analysts so that they can share experience. As a result, this is the model we are least likely to endorse.

Beneath the surface, each of these models is essentially either centralized or decentralized. The consulting and functional models are variations on centralization. The consulting model has different funding and deployment methods, and the functional model is centralized, just not at corporate. The CoE model is an overlay on a decentralized structure. So are other hybrid models, most commonly a combination of decentralized analyst groups in business units plus a central group at corporate that focuses on cross-functional, cross-organizational, and enterprise-wide initiatives.

These five models have pros and cons and trade-offs in terms of deployment and development and other objectives. Figure 11.2 shows the strengths of each in terms of four specific goals.

	Centralized	Consulting	Functional	CoE	Decentralized
Deploy analysts on the most important business initiatives	●		◐	◐	
Deploy analysts close to the business for purposes of service, responsiveness and local learning		◐	◐	●	●
Maximize the overall learning and development of analysts	●	◐		◐	
Maximize the engagement of analysts	●		◐	◐	

● = very strong

◐ = somewhat strong

Figure 11.2 Strengths of the five organizational models.

Coordination Approaches

One basic structure may be the best general fit, but no model will be best in terms of meeting all goals. Whatever the basic model, there will be a need to coordinate across analyst groups or across different parts of the business that are consuming analyst services. In a sense, all models are hybrids. Even if all analysts work in one centralized corporate unit, the customers for their services are spread across the enterprise. You need coordination mechanisms to manage and meet demand for analytics.

There are a variety of common coordination mechanisms, some of which we've already mentioned. These mechanisms can supplement the formal reporting structure for the purposes of enabling groups to plan and work together and developing an enterprise view of priorities and resources. Think of them as ways to supplement and fine-tune a basic centralized or decentralized model, or to compensate for its inherent weaknesses.

- **Program management office.** This is a formal corporate unit for setting enterprise priorities, coordinating analytics initiatives, influencing resource deployment on key initiatives, and facilitating the borrowing of staff across analytics groups. As mentioned, it may be a function within a CoE. PMOs are especially useful where potential business value is high and resources are scarce and distributed. Under a PMO, the deployment process must be sophisticated to meet the dual needs of project staffing and analyst development.

- **Federation.** Analyst groups and their associated business units work together on priorities, coordination of initiatives, resource deployment, and analyst development under a set of "guidelines of federation." The most basic form of federation is a clearly chartered enterprise governance or steering committee. These committees add an immediate enterprise view, but they sometimes lack clout and even commitment.

- **Community.** Decentralized analysts can be encouraged to share ideas and analytical approaches in a community. Such a community typically would involve occasional meetings, seminars, written communications, or electronic discussions or portals. It may be facilitated by a community organizer, and it typically benefits from a budget.

- **Matrix.** Analyst groups report both to their associated business units and to a corporate analytics unit, with one line solid and the other dotted. Establishing dotted-line reporting to a central organization injects an imperative to get coordinated, but dotted lines can lose their force over time if they're not regularly exercised.

- **Rotation.** Some of the analysts in a centralized model are physically located in and dedicated to business units on a rotational basis. Or an enterprise-wide program facilitates the lending and migration of analysts across decentralized units. The strength and success of rotation programs are easy to gauge. Analysts really do have mobility across the enterprise.

- **Assigned customers.** Some centralized analytics groups, such as the one at Procter & Gamble, have assigned analysts to work exclusively with particular business units and the leaders of those units. The assignments fall short of a matrixed tie in the organizational structure, but they help ensure that the analytical needs of the units and their leaders are met.

For purposes of deploying analysts on the most important business initiatives, the PMO is the strongest mechanism. For purposes of developing analysts, all the mechanisms can help the cause, and rotation programs have the most profound effect. The coordination mechanisms can be used in combination. Examples include a PMO focused on deployment and a community focused on development, or a federation focused on coordination and a matrix focused on ensuring alignment with business needs.

What Model Fits Your Business?

Any basic organizational design for analysts may look good on paper, but it's got to work in the context of how the business already operates. To evaluate, design, implement, and refine organizational structures, you've got to look behind the org chart and consider some basic variables that must work together for any organizational model to succeed. Figure 11.3 shows six key variables,[3] described in the following list.

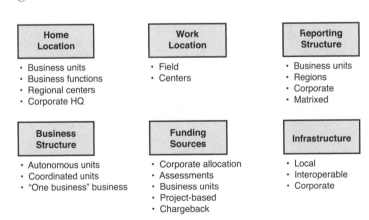

Figure 11.3 Organizational design variables.

- **Home location** is where analyst groups officially reside for administrative purposes—in business units or functions, regional centers, corporate headquarters, or some mix of these locations. Home base and formal reporting lines have been the dominant variables in organizational design, especially in companies where more headcount has indicated more power. However, in today's more fluid and collaborative organizations, home location means less and less (especially if coordination mechanisms are effective). Home location is a matter of convenience, with the goals of limiting travel to work locations, accommodating employees' preferences, and getting enough people in one place regularly to sustain a community.

- **Work location** is where the work of business analytics is performed, typically a mix of in the field (wherever the business customers of analytical models and services may be) and in regional or corporate analytics centers (where colleagues and support services are readily available). We find it best to locate analytics work, wherever possible, where the corresponding business work is. Make sure that home location and reporting structure don't erect barriers to analysts' working close to the business.

- **Reporting structure** is the formal lines of connection, direction, and administration. Analysts and their groups typically report to local business units, to corporate, or to an intermediate unit (such as business sector or region) if the corporation is so structured. Some reporting structures are a matrix, with analysts reporting solid-line to business units and dotted-line to the corporate analytics organization, or vice versa. Reporting structure may be predetermined if analytics is part of another organization, such as marketing or IT. Make sure that reporting lines are not so rigid as to impede the flexible staffing and development of analysts. Given the advantages of enterprise coordination of analytics, at least a dotted line to corporate makes sense in most organizations.

- **Business structure** is the shape of the enterprise. Are its business units highly autonomous? Or are they closely coordinated? To what extent do business units already share functions, services, and important-but-scarce resources? Is power concentrated at the regional level? Centralizing analysts may seem the logical thing to do. But it can prove impractical if that flies in the face of a locally autonomous or regionalized business structure.

Centralized analytics groups are a natural match for an integrated "one business" business. If business units are intertwined and must work with and rely on one another regularly, you need a centralized or consulting model, or else a strong federation.

If business units are autonomous, with little interconnection, analysts may stay decentralized, but a center of excellence helps in sharing experience and building the analyst community. And if the enterprise relies extensively on business partners to perform major processes, you may need a centralized structure, especially if there is a need or opportunity to coordinate analytics with partners.

- **Funding sources** are seldom considered in the context of organizational design, even though paralysis is guaranteed if organizational structure and funding sources are at odds. Friction is minimal if funding follows the lines of formal reporting, but matters are seldom that simple because business services such as analytics often have multiple funding sources. These may include funds from corporate, business unit assessments, direct funds from business units, chargeback to business units for analyst time, and project-based funding from the sponsoring business unit or units. The organizational questions are as follows: To what extent does the basic model under consideration align with funding sources? How does funding need to be revised or influenced by coordination mechanisms to support the analytics organization and its work?

  Project-based funding is the most market- and demand-driven, but it requires a certain level of maturity among business customers in setting analytics ambitions and priorities, and among analyst groups in advising customers and marketing their services. We recommend that project-based funding (or other funding for services performed) be supplemented by seed funding (to foster innovation) and infrastructure funding (to build capability), usually from corporate.

- **Infrastructure** includes the configuration and ownership of other essential resources, especially technology and data. This variable is similar to funding sources. Alignment is essential to the success, but the variable is seldom considered in organizational design. Analysts cannot work across business processes and units if local systems and databases, inconsistent tools, and fragmented infrastructure prevent it. And business units cannot incorporate new technologies and techniques for analytical applications if corporate standards prevent it. To capitalize on analytics, the infrastructure must be local-but-interoperable or corporate-but-flexible.

As a practical matter, these six variables are never perfectly aligned with each other, so you'll have to experiment with and adjust the coordination mechanisms over time. As a common example, if data and technical infrastructure are fragmented, you might phase in an organizational consolidation alongside (or slightly in advance of) the rationalization and consolidation of those resources.

How Bold Can You Be?

How aggressive should you be in your organizational design, especially in terms of consolidating and coordinating existing analyst groups? Sometimes "dropping in" a new centralized organizational structure sends a strong and positive signal. Other times it backfires and causes a backlash because the variables aren't aligned and the business units aren't ready. The most sensible path may be an organizational migration—consolidating groups, changing reporting lines, and layering on coordination mechanisms as analytical capability and maturity grow.

Before you proceed with connecting those "pockets of analytics" and consolidating analyst groups, assess how much leverage for consolidation you have (or lack). Consider two variables:

- **Analytical orientation** is the desire and capability of the various parts of the business to use analytics and manage by fact.
- **Enterprise commitment** is the desire and capability of the various parts of the business to work together as an enterprise and to compete on analytics.

As shown in Figure 11.4,[4] if both factors are high, you can probably bring together analytics groups directly through reporting structure. If analytical orientation is high and enterprise commitment is low, coordination mechanisms can be introduced in turn to build enterprise perspective and commitment. Most companies lead with a CoE to form a community of analysts and then follow with a governance committee to build consensus.

If enterprise commitment is high but analytical orientation is low, an investment in data and technology infrastructure can enable pilots and basic applications that demonstrate the possibilities. Create pockets of analytics with the intention of later combining them. And if both factors are low, the proponents of analytics need to find and build on local successes and spread the word to generate interest. The organizational issues of analytics are down the road.

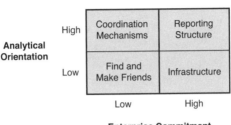

Figure 11.4 Analytical orientation and enterprise commitment.

Triangulating on Your Model and Coordination Mechanisms

You can zero in on or refine your organizational model for analysts by looking at the problem from a variety of angles and asking the right questions.

Angle 1: Current State

Most enterprises, especially those with low analytical maturity, have "pockets" of analytics in various places—a decentralized and fragmented structure. The first step in coordinating and consolidating is to inventory where analysts are, the kinds of things they're working on, and how they're connected and coordinated (if at all). Given the short-term analytical aspirations of the enterprise, what are the pros and cons of the current state? As discussed earlier, how much can you reasonably expect to consolidate and coordinate?

Angle 2: Analytical Maturity

Quickly assess your corporation against the five-stage maturity model (introduced in *Competing on Analytics*, detailed in *Analytics at Work*,[5] and shown in Figure 11.5). Note the common pattern in organizational evolution:

- Stage 1 and 2 companies tend to be decentralized.
- As ambition grows and becomes specific around Stage 3, the organization centralizes, and the functional model may serve for a time.
- Stages 4 and 5 have strong central organizations.

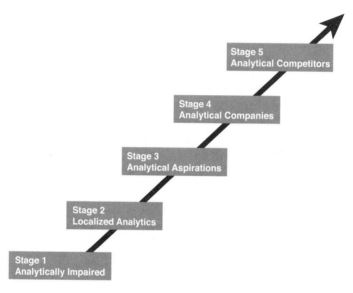

Figure 11.5 The five-stage maturity model.

The coordination mechanisms similarly evolve:

- At Stages 2 and 3, a center of excellence can build and add coherence to analyst capability.
- At Stage 3 or 4, a program office can focus the deployment of resources.
- At Stage 4 or 5, a formal federation may be necessary if the basic structure still has decentralized groups.

Ask yourself the following questions: What is the likely structure given our company's level of maturity? If ours needs to be different, why? And what other adjustments do we need to make?

Angle 3: Analytics Strategy/Scenario

Table 11.1 describes seven scenarios[6] for how enterprises approach and employ analytics. These different emphases suggest different basic organizational models.

Table 11.1 Ways in Which Enterprises Approach and Employ Analytics

Scenario	Definition	Basic Model
Traditional analytics and BI	Makes analytics tools and resources available to meet a broad variety of business needs	Centralized
Analytics for the masses	"Democratizes" analytics and spreads their use broadly across the organization	Centralized
Nonstandard data	Taps the analytical potential of unstructured and nonquantitative data	Functional if one unit is in the lead leveraging this data; otherwise, consulting or centralized
Decision-centered	Enables the rapid and accurate execution of business decisions, both frequent/structured and infrequent/new	The model is relatively unimportant as long as there's a means of sharing methods and experience
Embedded analytics	Makes real-time, automated analytical decisions part of core business processes and systems	Centralized or consulting
Function- or process-specific analytics	Uses specialized analytical technologies and applications to excel at a differentiating business process	Functional if an organization is focused on the process; otherwise, consulting or centralized
Industry-specific analytics	Uses specialized analytical technologies and applications to excel at processes common to an industry	Centralized or consulting, or functional if the focus is specific applications

Angle 4: Ambition Check

Consider what the enterprise wants to do with analytics and what it will take to succeed:

- **What are the next targets and opportunities?** If they are cross-functional, this may call for a more centralized basic model and/or additional coordination mechanisms. If they are process-specific, a temporary "best home" model may suggest itself.

- **How urgently does the enterprise need to build analytical capability?** More urgency calls for a more centralized model. So does heavy reliance on outside expertise. A center of excellence builds capability less rapidly.

- **How important is it to generate and manage demand for analytics across the enterprise?** Generating demand may call for "consultative sales" or "seeding" analysts across the enterprise. Managing and focusing demand that's already there may call for a program office or federation.

Angle 5: Reality Check

What organizational models work in your enterprise? What has been the experience with centralized staff functions and shared services organizations? With corporate consulting groups? Are there precedents for the functional, or "best home," model? What have been the pros and cons of these models in the past, and what will it take for them to succeed today in the analytics realm?

What has been the experience coordinating across decentralized groups? What has been your specific experience with each of the coordination mechanisms? For example, do your company's steering and governance committees succeed in enabling coordination, or are they usually limited to information exchange and advisory roles? Which coordination mechanisms can be relied upon? Have any developed a "bad rep?" What needs to be done differently for them to work in the analytics realm?

Finally, revisit the pragmatic constraints imposed by business structure, funding sources, and infrastructure. These variables are not very malleable, especially in the short term.

Analytical Leadership and the Chief Analytics Officer

Another key organizational question is the leadership role for analytics within organizations. Even though few official "Chief Analytics Officers (CAOs)" exist thus far, we expect that more will emerge. The role may not always have that title, but there is a need—at least for each of the three centrally coordinated models described earlier—for someone to lead the analytics organization. The CAO could be either a permanent role or a transitional role for an organization wanting to improve its analytical capabilities.

A Chief Analytics Officer's tasks could include any or all of the following:

- Mobilizing the needed data, people, and systems to make analytics succeed within an organization
- Working closely with executives to inject analytics into company strategies and important decisions
- Supervising the activities and careers of analytical people
- Consulting with business functions and units on how to take advantage of analytics in their business processes
- Surveying and contracting with external providers of analytical capabilities

One key issue for the CAO role is whether analytical people across the organization should report to it. Although an indirect reporting relationship (as one dimension of a matrixed organization) may be feasible, a CAO without any direct or indirect reports seems unlikely to be effective.

In one insurance firm, for example, the CEO was passionate about the role of analytics and named a CAO as a direct report. But the CAO had only a couple of staff; all other analytics people in the organization did not report to him. The CEO did not want to rock the organizational boat by having such traditional analytical functions in insurance as actuaries and underwriters report to the CAO. As a result, the CAO felt he had no ability to carry out his objectives. He resigned from the role, and the CEO did not replace him.

To Where Should Analytical Functions Report?

There are a variety of different places in the organization to which centralized analytical groups and their CAO leaders can report. Although there is no ideal reporting relationship, each one has its strengths and weaknesses:

- **Information technology.** Some organizations, such as a leading consumer products firm, have built analytical capabilities within the IT organization or have transferred them there. There are several reasons why this reporting relationship makes sense:

  - Analytics are heavily dependent on both data and software, and expertise in both of these is most likely to reside in an IT function.

  - The IT function is used to serving a wide variety of organizational functions and business units.

  - Analytics are closely aligned with some other typical IT functions, such as business intelligence and data warehousing.

  Of course, there are some disadvantages as well. IT organizations are sometimes slow to deliver analytical capabilities and may have a poor reputation as a result. They may also overemphasize the technical components of analytics and not focus sufficiently on business, organization, behavior, skill, and culture-related issues. Finally, IT organizations typically want to produce standardized and common solutions, and this may inhibit one-off analytical projects. In principle, however, there is no reason why IT organizations cannot overcome these problems.

- **Strategy.** A few analytical groups, including those at a large retailer, report to a corporate strategy organization. This relationship allows analysts to become privy to the organization's key strategic initiatives and objectives. Another virtue is that strategy groups are often staffed by analytically focused MBAs who may understand and appreciate analytical work, even if they cannot perform it themselves. The possible downsides of this reporting relationship are that strategy groups may be unable to marshal the technical and data resources to make analytical projects succeed, and strategy groups are usually relatively small.

- **Shared services.** In organizations with a shared administrative services organization, an analytics group can simply be part of that capability. That's where analytics reside, for example, in an Asia-based telecom company. The primary benefit of such a reporting structure is that analysts can serve anyone in the company—and often charging and resource allocation mechanisms are in place for doing so. The downside is that analytics may be viewed as a low-value, nonstrategic resource like some other shared service functions. With the appropriate mechanisms in place, this problem can surely be avoided.

- **Finance.** Being numbers-focused, finance organizations have the potential to be a home for business analytics groups. The obvious advantage of this arrangement would be the ability to focus analytics on the issues that matter most to business performance, including enterprise performance management itself. But for some unknown reason, most CFOs have not embraced analytics, and the finance function remains a logical, if uncommon, home for analytical groups. At some firms, however, including Caesar's Entertainment and Darden Restaurants, the finance function is beginning to play a much stronger role in championing analytical projects and perspectives. Caesar's has created a shared analytical services group reporting through the CFO.

- **Marketing or another specific function.** As noted, if an organization's primary analytical activities are concentrated within marketing or some other specific function, it makes sense to incorporate the analytical group within it. The resulting structure would allow a close focus on the analytics applications and issues in the functional area. Obviously, this would also make it more difficult for analytical initiatives outside those functional areas to be pursued.

Building an Analytical Ecosystem

Most of the foregoing discussion about analytical capabilities has focused on organizing and developing internal analytical capabilities. But a broad set of analytical offerings are made available by a wide variety of external providers as well. These providers include consultants, IT (primarily software) vendors, offshore analytical outsourcers, data providers, and other categories of assistance. Some provide general analytical help across industries, but almost every industry also has specialized analytics and data providers.

The key in constructing an effective analytical ecosystem is not to let it grow at random, but to identify the analytical capabilities the organization needs overall. Then you should decide whether internal or external capabilities are more appropriate to fill a specific need. In general, external capabilities make sense when the need is highly specialized, not likely to be needed frequently, and not critical to the organization's ongoing analytical capabilities.

A major pharmaceutical firm's Commercial Analytics group, for example, has a well-developed ecosystem. This is a large group of internal analysts (more than 30), but their abilities are supplemented by outside help when necessary. The group has worked with specialized consultants to analyze physician targeting, for example. The company's primary prescription data provider also works with it on analytics issues. Software vendors have consulted on analytical methods and techniques. Finally, the group supplements its work with help from an offshore analytics vendor in India.

Developing the Analytical Organization Over Time

A final point is that analytical organization structures should develop and evolve over time. An internal structure and ecosystem that make sense at the beginning of developing analytical capabilities will become obsolete later. For example, it may be reasonable to have a highly decentralized organizational model early on, but most firms create mechanisms for coordination and collaboration around analytics as they mature in their analytical orientations. It may also make sense to "borrow" a number of external resources in a firm's early stages of analytical maturity before committing to building internal capabilities.

The best way to adapt organizational capabilities to current needs is with a strategy or plan. Admittedly, in the early stages, the organization may not have anyone with the formal authority to even create a plan. However, if it appears that analytics will be key to an organization's future, it may make sense for a small group of analysts to get together and create a plan from the bottom up.

At a large U.S. bank, for example, the head of the distribution organization (including physical branches, call centers, ATMs, and online channels) had a large number of analysts in her organization. But she believed they weren't providing the value of which they were capable. She met with the managers of the diverse analytics and reporting groups in her business unit and asked one of them to take the lead in assessing the problem. His work determined that the vast majority of the groups worked on reports rather than more predictive analytics and that virtually no resources were devoted to cross-channel analytics. With this start, the group began to develop a plan to remedy the situation and shift the balance toward predictive analytics and a cross-channel perspective.

Plans should probably be revised every year or so, or when major changes occur in the demand or supply around analytics. There are usually clear signs—if anyone is looking—that the current model has become dysfunctional. It's a key step in an organization's analytical development for someone to take responsibility—either informally or formally—for assessing the organization for analytical resources and creating a better model.

No plan or organizational structure is perfect, even for a given time and situation. Every structure, if taken beyond its limits, will become a limitation. The leaders of contemporary organizations need to become conversant with their analytical capabilities and how they are organized. Most importantly, they need to realize when their current organizational approach no longer functions effectively and needs to be restructured.

The Bottom Line

The structure of your analyst organization cannot be slave to the company's other structures and methods, but it cannot operate in defiance of them, either. If your company is large and complex, odds are your analyst organization will be a hybrid—somewhat decentralized to reflect the shape of the business, but more centralized than the business at large. That means you'll rely on coordination mechanisms that must simultaneously serve the analytical interests of business units and the enterprise. The ideal may be a strong federation where the parties are collectively motivated to take an enterprise approach to analytics, including prioritizing, funding, and staffing cross-functional and enterprise-wide projects.

Endnotes

1. "Counting on Analytical Talent," Accenture Institute for High Performance, 2010.

2. Thomas H. Davenport, Jeanne G. Harris, and Robert Morison, *Analytics at Work: Smarter Decisions, Better Results*, Harvard Business Press, 2010. See pages 104–109.

3. This framework is based on "Building an Analytical Organization," The Business Analytics Concours and nGenera Corporation, 2008.

4. Ibid.

5. Thomas H. Davenport and Jeanne G. Harris, *Competing on Analytics: The New Science of Winning*, Harvard Business Press, 2007. See pages 35–40. Thomas H. Davenport, Jeanne G. Harris, and Robert Morison, *Analytics at Work: Smarter Decisions, Better Results*, Harvard Business Press, 2010. See Appendix, pages 185–188.

6. This framework is based on "Mastering the Technologies of Business Analytics," The Business Analytics Concours and nGenera Corporation, 2008.

12

Engaging Analytical Talent

Jeanne G. Harris and Elizabeth Craig

If your company is like a growing number of others, it's turning to analytics in search of a competitive edge. Your success with analytics hinges on your ability to effectively understand and engage analytical talent—employees who use statistics, rigorous quantitative and qualitative analysis, and information-modeling techniques to shape and make business decisions. First, of course, it's important to understand the different types of analysts and how common each is in the company.

Four Breeds of Analytical Talent

Drawing on our research with Tom Davenport and Bob Morison in *Competing on Analytics* and *Analytics at Work*, as well as our experience with dozens of analytically oriented companies across a broad range of industries, we've identified four types of analytical talent. Successful analytical organizations depend on these types of talent to achieve and sustain a competitive edge:

- **Sponsors** are senior executives who lead business initiatives and depend on data and analysis as core inputs into business decisions.

- **Scientists** (sometimes called data scientists) are the chief architects of analytical applications, developing statistical models and algorithms used by others in the organization for a range of business-related analyses. They also employ advanced data visualization capabilities to represent and interpret big data sets.

- **Experts** quantitatively oriented professionals with advanced functional and industry expertise. They are responsible for running analyses and applying analytics to solve complex business problems.

- **Users** are employees from any level of the organization who combine basic data analysis with business insights to use analytical insights in their work.

These types are illustrated in Figure 12.1, where the percentages represent the proportions of different types of analytical talent in a typical organization.

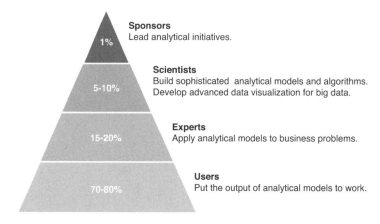

Sponsors
Lead analytical initiatives.

Scientists
Build sophisticated analytical models and algorithms. Develop advanced data visualization for big data.

Experts
Apply analytical models to business problems.

Users
Put the output of analytical models to work.

1%
5-10%
15-20%
70-80%

Figure 12.1 Types of analysts.

Sponsors are important. They provide the leadership, direction, and impetus required to execute analytical strategies. They're few and far between. Users are also important. They rely on data and analytics to perform their everyday jobs. But it's the Scientists and Experts who constitute the lifeblood of your analytical organization: They create and use complex analytical applications to benefit the business, and they possess rare, valuable, and specialized skills.

Engaging Analysts

Even if you have all of these different types of analysts, chances are you don't really know how to make sure analysts are energized by, enthusiastic about, and engrossed in their work. In other words, how do you keep these scarce and valuable workers engaged so that they help your company succeed?

The business literature is rife with studies on how to engage employees, but analysts are different from other workers. They have distinct backgrounds, skills, attitudes, and motivations. Established practices for engaging employees—such as providing meaningful work and career opportunities—matter to analysts too. But you must also attend to analysts' unique needs. If you fail to do so, analysts may not invest their full physical, mental, and emotional energies into their work.

To help your organization avoid this mistake, it's critical to understand the unique factors that influence analysts' engagement. To discern these factors, we interviewed dozens of executives and surveyed 1,367 employees to better understand what matters to analysts. We examined more than 30 factors believed to affect employee engagement, including company culture, leadership, organizational systems, management practices, career opportunities, and coworker relationships.

The good news is that analysts are significantly more engaged at work than other types of employees. Overall, 57% of analysts reported being moderately or highly engaged, compared with 45% of other employees. But there's bad news, too: Nearly one in four analysts simply go through the motions. They show up for work each day, but they don't give their all. And another 20% of our respondents were completely disengaged. For companies that rely on data-driven insights, those stats should be alarming.

Like all employees, analysts are most engaged by work that allows them to apply their skills and talents, gain valuable experience, and contribute to the organization's overall goals. However, several things are uniquely important to analysts. They need to understand the wider business as well as analytics, they need to know exactly what is expected of them, and they need to have opportunities keep their technical skills and expertise up to date. Human Resources has a vital role to play in tailoring practices to analysts' unique engagement needs.

Arm Analysts with Critical Information About the Business

As analytics become more integral to a company's strategy, analysts need the business knowledge and skills to enable them to understand the strategic issues facing the company and how analytics can be used to drive business value. Not only does insight into the business make analysts more effective, but it also boosts their engagement. In fact, it's one of the strongest predictors of analyst engagement. In our research, analysts who understand their company's strategy, goals, capabilities, and operations were three times more likely to be highly engaged than analysts who don't have a firm grasp of the business. Moreover, analysts who understand how their work relates to their organization's goals and contributes to its success were nearly six times more likely to be highly engaged than those who don't.

The best managers expose analysts to a range of business units and functions so that they learn about the company's main business challenges and work processes. Leaders at one global financial services company we studied stressed the need for analysts to understand the business so that they can identify opportunities for analytics to have an impact on the organization's results. Managers give analysts the tools and templates they need to capture business strategy, define problems, and devise solutions. This helps analysts communicate effectively with business leaders, because they can explain how their work creates value for the firm.

Colin Sheppard, formerly Virgin Media's Director of Knowledge and Insight, says that Virgin trains its analysts to think like clients. He finds that not only are the best analysts technically outstanding, but they also understand the consumer's key motivations and are focused on commercial objectives. Analysts who can confidently communicate their findings (for example, which customers are most likely to buy a new product or service) in terms important to senior executives were six times more likely to be highly engaged. They're also more likely to persuade management to act on their recommendations.

Define Roles and Expectations

It's frustrating when you don't know what you're supposed to do. Engagement suffers in the absence of clear goals and expectations—and this is especially true for analytical talent. Research has shown that, as a group, people with a strong quantitative orientation tend to be less tolerant of uncertainty and think in a more linear fashion. That's why they are so good at what they do: They can turn raw data into clear insights by creating models and applications that make sense of it. That penchant for order leads analysts to prefer structured and predictable work environments. In our study, analysts who said they are clear about their roles were six times more likely to be highly engaged. The flip side? Analysts with ambiguous roles were *nine* times more likely to be disengaged.

At Google, employees know what's expected of them. Roles are highly structured according to a 70/20/10 model. Employees spend 70% of their time fulfilling basic job requirements, 20% on projects that help them develop technical skills and benefit the company, and 10% on product and business innovations. Although aspects of the role are open-ended, overall expectations, job requirements, and performance metrics are clearly defined.

Role clarity is particularly important for engaging the most quantitative-minded analysts. Analytical scientists are much more likely to be engaged when they have a clear understanding of their responsibilities, objectives, and authority. Three out of four analytical scientists we surveyed who know what's expected of them were highly engaged, compared with just one in ten who lack such clarity.

Clear does not mean rote, however. Analysts place a premium on interesting and challenging work. They want to work with a variety of datasets and types of analyses. One grocery retailer could not effectively retain employees assigned to perform an essential but repetitive analysis. The company could attract highly skilled MBAs to the job, but it could not keep them for long. The analysts quickly became restless and sought new challenges. Variety in their work keeps analysts engaged.

Feed Analysts' Love of New Techniques, Tools, and Technologies

Analytical work requires specialized skills, and skill requirements change rapidly as new analytical tools and techniques emerge. Opportunities to keep their technical skills up to date are vital to keeping analysts engaged. This is especially true for analytical scientists. Scientists who said they can keep up with the latest analytic models, tools, and technologies in their field were *26 times* more likely to be highly engaged than those who cannot.

Consider the statisticians at AT&T Labs. The mandate of this analytical talent is "to develop new methodologies to deal with large-scale data problems—the type of problems generated by the massive stores of data AT&T collects to run its business," says Chris Volinsky, director of the Statistics Research Department. To do this, it's essential that they keep up with the latest advances in statistical theory and methodology. One way these analytical scientists do so is by pursuing problems across the business and beyond. A few years ago, the group took on a challenge posed by Netflix, the online DVD-rental company, and won. Netflix offered a top prize of $1 million to anyone who could improve—by at least 10%—the accuracy of Cinematch, its movie recommendation algorithm.

Volinsky and an AT&T Labs colleague teamed up with five others from outside the organization to win the competition—three years after it began. "When we started working on it," Volinsky says, "it wasn't obvious what the tie-in was to AT&T." But the company supported their participation anyway. And in the end, AT&T was also a winner: "The algorithms that we developed for the Netflix prize have benefited our research here," says Volinsky.

He adds, "That freedom to start working on it in the first place was a function of the culture that we have here." That culture allows AT&T to make sure its top quant talent is constantly expanding their technical expertise—and to engage and retain world-class analytical talent.

Employ More Centralized Analytical Organization Structures

The survey data suggest that if you care about having your analysts engaged with their jobs and hope they remain in your employ, the two most successful organizational models in that regard are the *center of excellence (CoE)* (29% engaged, 41% likely to stay) and *centralized* (35% engaged, 33% likely to stay) models (see Chapter 11 for descriptions of these). The percentages for the more decentralized models are clearly worse on both measures. The *decentralized* model had only 18% of analysts engaged and 27% likely to stay.

We found that analysts in centralized units and centers of excellence are most engaged and most likely to stay because they enjoy the most meaningful career opportunities. Three key factors influence the quality of analysts' work and career opportunities and, in turn, drive engagement and retention (see Figure 12.2):

- Analysts' work is aligned with the organization's strategy and goals and affects its success (they are engaged in significant work for the company).
- Analysts understand the dynamics of the industry and business model (business insight).
- Analysts' skills and aspirations are a good match with the company's culture and goals (organizational fit).

Lacking the opportunity to make a real impact on the organization's success, analysts won't find enough meaning in their work, so they will be less engaged and less likely to stay. Perhaps the biggest demotivator for analytical scientists is spending too much time on simple analyses and report generation instead of building and refining analytical models. We know of several organizations that have lost analysts who felt they were treated largely as "spreadsheet developers." It's essential to give your best analysts opportunities to apply their expertise to the company's biggest problems.

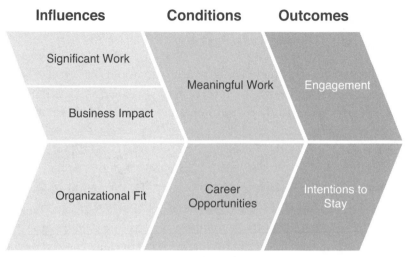

Copyright © 2011 Accenture All Rights Reserved.

Figure 12.2 Factors that influence the quality of analysts' work and job opportunities.

Unfortunately, even the best organizational models are somewhat low in engagement and intent to stay. These analysts are incredibly valuable to any company pursuing a data- and analysis-based strategy. Companies need to find ways to make their analyst jobs more fulfilling if they hope to retain their most valuable analysts.

When employers keep analytical talent engaged, everyone wins. Analysts relish their work, and their companies build analytical capabilities and bolster their long-term competitiveness. By honing their awareness of analysts' distinct engagement needs, human resources leaders, executives, and managers can help lay the foundation for a fully engaged analytical workforce.

13

Governance for Analytics

Stacy Blanchard and Robert Morison

Whenever an organization develops new capability, questions of guidance and authority arise. If the questions are not addressed and resolved quickly, avoidable problems surface, the capability is ineffectively deployed, and business benefits are diluted and delayed. The policies and processes of *governance* address how to define and manage a capability and its resources. Governance facilitates organizational alignment, cultural support, and high performance as the capability is deployed.

Such is the case as organizations today build their capability in business analytics. Strong governance can accelerate progress and amplify results, thus improving decision-making and business performance within and across business units, optimizing processes more broadly, and focusing analytics on strategic goals. Under weak governance, analytics efforts are fragmented and they underperform. Ambitions and priorities are unclear; resources can be squandered on low-value projects; data, technology, and skills are unavailable when needed; and nobody has real ownership or accountability for results.

Establishing governance is a mix of science and art, where the specific power dynamics within the organization play a significant role. There is no single right governance model for analytics, but a number of good principles and practices are commonly found among organizations with high-performing analytical capabilities.

Guiding Principles

We recommend starting with a set of principles guiding the business use of analytics—and thus the design of a governance model for analytics. Principles establish basic direction, ground rules, and expectations. Useful principles aren't about good intentions that everyone can readily subscribe to. Rather, they drive choices among alternatives. They carry implications, including for what the enterprise chooses *not* to do. A different enterprise will have a very different set of principles.

The process of developing guiding principles should surface important (even contentious) issues, enabling debate and then alignment. As soon as an executive team and other stakeholders agree to follow a set of principles, everyday decisions are more straightforward; further debate about things such as objectives, priorities, and resource allocations has context; and resolution comes more quickly.

The following are some common categories for principles guiding business analytics, with a sample principle for each. Note that these principles are not specifically recommended, nor are they intended to be a coherent set. They simply illustrate the kinds of principles organizations adopt around analytics. Think about the implications of each and about what variation or alternative principle might suit your enterprise in each category.

- **Ambition.** What does the enterprise seek to accomplish through analytics? Example: We will differentiate our business and achieve superior retention of customers and employees by applying analytics to customer service and talent management processes.
- **Scope.** How broadly across the enterprise will analytical tools and applications be deployed? Example: We will equip all business decision-makers and knowledge workers with useful data and analytical tools.
- **Enterprise.** What processes and resources will be managed at the enterprise level? Example: Data is owned by the corporation and managed enterprise-wide; business units may adapt

and supplement a standard analytics toolkit; analyst talent is locally managed but coordinated across the enterprise.

- **Leadership.** What responsibilities do business leaders have for using and enabling analytics? Example: The CEO and executive team are responsible for strategy and investment in analytics, as well as for building an analytical culture.

- **Governance.** How will the business set direction and manage performance of analytics? Example: A cross-functional governing body will determine targets for major analytics applications, allocate resources, and ensure communication and coordination across analytics initiatives.

- **Budget.** How will analytics resources be funded? Example: We will have a rolling three-year investment plan and budget for analytics data, infrastructure, and talent; analytics applications will be funded as business innovation projects.

- **Responsibility.** What are the expectations for use of analytics in the enterprise? Example: All managers and knowledge workers will be evaluated and rewarded for incorporating analytics into their work and decisions.

- **Culture.** What are the expectations for analytical behavior in the enterprise? Example: All employees should be familiar with available information and should be fact-based in their decisions and actions, and they should expect the same behaviors in others.

Elements of Governance

Effective governance entails more than establishing a governing body, even though that's the first thing most of us think of when we say "governance." A rigorous approach to governance incorporates purpose, scope, structure, roles and responsibilities, processes, and relationships across the enterprise—the six elements depicted in Figure 13.1. To establish effective governance of analytics (or any other business capability), you should address the six questions discussed in the following sections. Answer them initially with the help of your guiding principles and your organization's experience with governance. Then expect the answers to adjust as governing bodies gain experience and their charters evolve. Let's explore each of these elements in more detail.

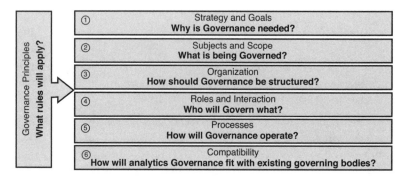

Figure 13.1 Elements of governance.

Why Is Governance Needed?

What is the business trying to accomplish through analytics? Improve the performance of key processes? Provide better information for specific classes of management decisions? Seek competitive advantage through analytical capabilities and applications? Are there cross-functional opportunities for performance improvements, but you need to bridge organizational silos to put analytics to work? Are parts of the business adept at analytics, and you want to spread that capability to other areas? Is there a lot of localized analytics activity, so you need to coordinate resources and priorities?

Your goals for analytics—and therefore for the shape of analytics governance—are based on business ambitions, the current state of analytical capability, and the readiness of the business to become more analytical and work in new ways. Goals may be ambitious, but they should also be realistic, grounded in the current maturity level of the enterprise. Using the five-stage maturity model from Davenport and Harris's book *Competing on Analytics* (see Figure 13.2), assess where the enterprise is today, what it takes to move to the next level, and what the ultimate ambition may be.

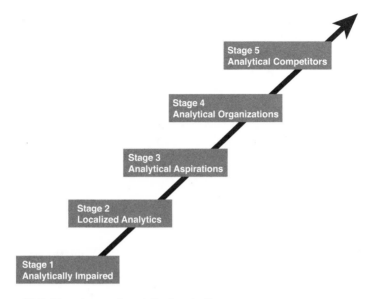

Figure 13.2 Five stages of analytical maturity.

You will find many opportunities to put analytics to work—too many to pursue all at once. Governance is needed to set priorities, manage resources and investments, and, above all, ensure that analytical efforts are in pursuit of business strategy. Analytics can be a powerful tool in many business decisions, such as which companies to merge with or acquire, where to strategically place new locations, or what demand to expect for the next product or service innovation. Governance should align analytics to your enterprise's unique strategy and goals.

- **Stage 1: Analytically impaired.** Initially, there may be little awareness of, or appetite or capability for, analytics in the organization.
- **Stage 2: Localized analytics.** There are pockets of interest and activity, and some local applications and databases, but no large-scale commitment to or leverage of, business analytics.
- **Stage 3: Analytical aspirations.** The enterprise starts to get serious. Leaders look for analytics-based business opportunities. Applications become more cross-functional and valuable. The enterprise invests more systematically in data and analytics infrastructure.

- **Stage 4: Analytical organizations.** The business has turned the corner and now uses analytics regularly in making decisions and executing and improving business processes. Analytics are a regular part of the toolkit. Not everyone is analytical, but the enterprise recognizes and rewards those who are.

- **Stage 5: Analytical competitors.** The company uses analytics not just in everyday work, but to differentiate itself in the marketplace. The analytical competitor very purposefully deploys analytics in its most strategically important business activities and initiatives.

What Is Being Governed?

What is the scope of analytics governance? What resources are in its purview? What kinds of decisions do governing bodies make? What business activities are they attempting to influence? Governance may cover everything from the overall strategy for analytics to targets, investments, talent, infrastructure, and even culture. And for each subject of governance there must be boundaries, standards, guidelines, and realistic goals.

Specific subjects that analytics governance commonly addresses include the following:

- **Strategy and targets.** What is our overall business strategy for analytics? What are the most important target applications? And what are their business goals—revenue increases, cost reduction, market share, competitive advantage?

- **Investments.** How much should we spend on analytics initiatives and infrastructure, and what should the investment mix be across applications and organizations?

- **Infrastructure.** How well do the technical and data infrastructure support analytics? How consistent do they need to be across the enterprise?

- **Talent.** Does the enterprise have the right amount and mix of analytical talent—from professional model builders to executives, managers, knowledge workers, and process performers who can use analytics in their work and decisions? How should the talent pool be expanded?

- **Leadership.** Who should lead analytics initiatives and groups, and how well are they performing? Are business executives leading initiatives and modeling the right analytical behaviors?

- **Decision-making.** What types of strategic or operational business decisions should analytics focus on? How should the decision-making methods and style of the enterprise change for the better?

- **Culture.** Is the organization analytically oriented? Are decisions data-driven? Does it test and learn? Can people challenge one another for the data and analyses behind their opinions and actions?

Governance always addresses the coordination and management of analytics resources. A key question is whether it should also address the analytical capability of the enterprise at large. Should the charter include trying to influence the leadership behaviors, decision-making methods, and culture of the business? The charter may expand with analytical maturity, capability, and accomplishment. To gain initial momentum with analytics, governance focuses on essential resources and the success of selected initiatives. As analytics takes hold across the enterprise, governance may evolve to include not only how analytics are delivered, but also how effectively the business consumes and leverages them.

How Should Governance Be Structured?

There is not a one-size-fits-all approach to structuring analytics governance. However, most companies use steering committees for cross-functional governance of new capabilities, and that's a good place to start. More often than not, a two-tier committee structure will suffice. An overall leadership steering committee handles strategy and direction (and is the last word when issues arise). A series of tactical subcommittees focus on relevant subjects—targets, talent, infrastructure, data. The subcommittees "report to" the overall steering committee, providing an element of hierarchy. They also network with each other and perhaps occasionally convene en masse.

Key questions in establishing the right structure for analytics governance include the following:

- What deserves a focused subcommittee? Start with your answers to "What is being governed?" as discussed earlier.

- How much overlapping membership should the subcommittees have? If the challenges are interlocked ("We need additional talent to get our data in shape for analytics") or the organizations involved are just learning to work together, more overlaps are needed.

- Should there be sunset clauses so that committees disband when their work is done, rather than continuing to go through the motions? Set specific goals for each committee and revisit its charter when the goals are met.

Figure 13.3 depicts a representative two-tier structure, together with the business operations themselves, where the analytics work and projects get done.

Your structure for analytics governance also depends on the following:

- **The size and scale of the analytics program.** The size and complexity of the enterprise and its analytics function determine how much representation is needed on the various committees, as do the level and spread of analytics activity across the business. Smaller organizations with limited analytics activity can have simplified governance, perhaps just an overall steering committee to start. A large, complex, and diversified enterprise may need a third tier or parallel structure of committees by business unit.

- **Management style and organizational culture.** How does your organization make decisions and manage resources today? Is it consensus-based? Leadership-led? Majority rule? Your approach to governing analytics should start with what works in the organization—and not go too much against the grain of the management style and culture. For instance, if you have a flat organization with minimal hierarchy and bureaucracy, an overly complex and hierarchical governance structure would be unlikely to engage participation and support. A simple network of focused committees would be more appropriate.

- **Analytical maturity.** As analytical maturity increases through the early stages, the governance structure will likely expand to cover more subjects and establish the right mix of local and enterprise-wide responsibilities. Then, at higher levels of maturity where analytics have become institutionalized, the structure may streamline because there's less need for monitoring and intervention.

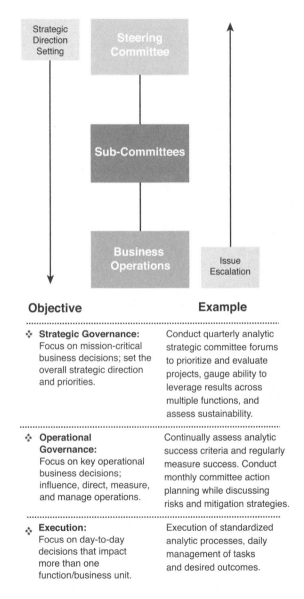

Figure 13.3 Sample governance structure.

Regardless of how you structure governance, make sure that the bodies have clear purpose and charters, the right stakeholder membership, and the authority to handle the strategic and operational issues of analytics.

Who Will Govern What?

However you structure governance for analytics, success hinges on having the necessary people participate and making decision rights clear for both governing bodies and individual managers. The starting question—and typically a source of tension and a matter of constant adjustment in the governance process—is what decisions and resources should be managed at the enterprise level versus in business units or other constituent organizations.

Each committee should include stakeholders from across the enterprise (or at least the parts of the enterprise with analytical activity). For example, a subcommittee on analytical talent may include representation from human resources, the lines of business, and the analytics organization's management. As a general rule, most committees should have representation from IT and the business.

Especially when moving up the analytics maturity curve, and managing new capabilities and resources, you can't be too precise about responsibilities and decision rights. Which committees are responsible for which decisions and resources, and when do they have to work together? What individuals—in business operations, the IT organization, and the analytics function—work with or "report to" each committee (even if they are not members)?

We recommend starting with a standard RACI analysis from the project management literature. For each category of resource or decision (again, the first cut will be the subjects of governance, as discussed earlier), specify who is:

- **R**esponsible for action
- **A**ccountable for results (the ultimate authority)
- **C**onsulted in the course of decision-making
- **I**nformed about decisions and actions

This stakeholder management helps clarify roles and responsibilities, identify key decision points, eliminate misunderstandings, encourage teamwork, reduce duplication of effort, and enable timely, consistent, and complete communication. When establishing decision rights, avoid these common pitfalls:

- Not getting full buy-in from all legitimate stakeholders.
- Neglecting day-to-day stakeholder management. Don't forget to involve the "Consults" and "Informs" regularly.
- Letting corporate authority override analytics accountability and the business hierarchy supplant the governance model.

Keep in mind that, if your organization has difficulty working cross-functionally, or confronting performance and accountability issues, it will take more than a governance model to shift behaviors. It may take specific accountabilities, performance measures, rewards, and consequences for the individuals participating in governance of analytics.

Governance of Descriptive Versus Predictive Analytics

Analytical emphasis shapes governance because descriptive and predictive analytics have different goals, resources, costs, and deployment tactics.

Descriptive analytics, often referred to as business intelligence (BI), focus primarily on historical data and "What happened?" Operational subject matter experts identify important questions and variables and build reports and management dashboards. The challenge often involves pulling together information from large datasets—providers, members, and claims in health insurance or customers, products, suppliers, and sales in retail.

Governance in a descriptive analytics environment focuses on the coordination and procedures required to ensure data quality and availability, as well as a standard data management platform and analytics and reporting toolkit. It may resemble traditional IT project portfolio management.

Advanced or predictive analytics, on the other hand, are aimed at determining what actions to take. For example, in customer retention, descriptive reports might show which stores have higher churn, while predictive analytics explore why and what to do about it. What customers are likely or unlikely to return, what factors shape their decisions, and what timely actions can turn dissatisfied customers into satisfied ones? Predictive analytics often involve new data combinations, including third-party data (such as consumer demographics or attitudes).

Governance for predictive analytics focuses more on how analytics are used to simulate business activities and support business decisions. At this higher level of analytical maturity, governance methods are much more focused on enabling experimentation and iterative model development. It may resemble research and development portfolio management.

How Will Governance Operate?

When people come together in new governing bodies, it helps to anticipate and outline the basic ways in which they will work. But keep in mind that these will evolve as the participants learn to work together and as the charters of the governing bodies change. Key processes for governance of analytics include the following:

- **Decision-making** is selecting a course of action from among proposed alternatives. The process of establishing decision rights includes examining the nature of key decisions. These vary in complexity and impact. Some require input from across the organization, and others can be made by designated groups or individuals. People should be clear about what decisions they're involved in and when and how quickly decisions need to be made. The decision-making style of the enterprise shapes this process for analytics.

- **Strategic planning and investment** is the periodic process of determining and adjusting an enterprise's strategy for using analytics, and allocating resources to pursue the strategy. This includes ensuring that the analytics strategy aligns with and promotes the overarching business strategy as the latter changes with marketplace conditions and ambitions. It also includes establishing the long-term investment plan for analytics infrastructure, data, and talent.

- **Target setting and approvals** involves determining what analytics applications and models to develop and where in the enterprise to deploy analytical tools. The targets for analytics should tie directly back to the business strategy, and the business case for each should specify goals. Keep in mind, however, the experimental nature of analytics applications—you learn as you go. Thus, goals should be expressed as a range and adjusted along the way. The approval process may look more like that for business innovation initiatives than that for well-specified IT projects. Whatever the process, stakeholders should perceive it as transparent and fair.

- **Performance management** is the ongoing monitoring, measurement, and improvement of the applications, models, and tools that have been deployed. Results should be measured in business terms—revenue, cost, share, and operational performance metrics (such as increasing sales to existing customers by 10%)—as well as in terms of the functionality and performance of analytics applications. Direct responsibility for results rests with the business operations using analytics, together with the analytics function. However, the governance committees must actively monitor results, both to gauge the impact and value of the overall analytics program and to advise and, as needed, intervene to help keep major initiatives on track.

- **Issue management.** Some issues are recognized by governance bodies in the course of monitoring performance and results. Others are raised by the people experiencing problems and conflicts in implementing analytics and enabling their business use. Either way, the governance committees need a transparent process for discussing and resolving the issues. Issue management includes the identification, classification, analysis, and timely resolution or further escalation of issues. There are two keys to success: anticipating what kinds of issues are likely to arise (such as conflicting priorities among organizations that need to cooperate) and resolving issues at the right level (such as resisting the temptation to escalate matters further).

How Will Analytics Governance Fit with Other Governance Bodies and Methods?

Analytics governance must be compatible with the enterprise's management style and methods, and it should try to follow the precedent of other successful cross-functional governance models in the organization. Analytics governance also has specific relationships with other governance bodies and methods wherever their domains overlap. It's useful to map these relationships, including points of interaction and what information is held in common or exchanged. As a design principle, interactions should be kept as simple as possible, and any new governance entity should leverage the information and methods of existing governance groups to get a head start and avoid duplication of effort. Figure 13.4 shows some of the common intersections between analytics governance and other governance bodies and methods.

What?	Who?	Possible Interactions	
Company Strategy	Strategic Steering Committee	Strategic goals and decisions ➡ ⬅ Strategic initiatives	
Strategic Maps and KPIs	Balanced Scorecard	Strategic alignment results ➡ ⬅ KPIs/outcomes produced	Analytical Governance Model
Programs and Projects	Program Mgmt Office(s)	Program management ➡ ⬅ Program tracking	
Budgeting	Functional Area	Budget tracking ➡ ⬅ Budget formulation	
Investments	Investment Committees	Project approvals ➡ ⬅ Project investment reqs	
Enterprise Architecture	Competency Center	Dimensions enablement ➡ ⬅ Dimensions definition	
Information Technology	IT Governance Board	IT standards ➡ ⬅ Orchestration	

Figure 13.4 Examples of governance relationships.

You Know You're Succeeding When...

How do you know that governance of analytics is working effectively? Look first, of course, at the business results of analytics initiatives. Do they deliver intended value in the intended time frame? Do they exceed their formal objectives by enabling the business to learn new things and ask better questions? Are they enabling the enterprise to become more rigorous and fact-based in its decision-making?

Then review the processes and behaviors of analytics governance and assess how smoothly things are running. The following are ten "litmus tests." You can tell analytics governance is working well when they occur:

- The most important and strategic business analytics initiatives have priority and resources.
- Participants in analytics governance are eager to work together. They don't try to delegate attendance at committee meetings.
- People have agreed to agree. They cite the guiding principles and cooperate and compromise accordingly. Committees don't get bogged down over priorities and resource allocations.
- Local interests don't prevail, and corporate hierarchy doesn't overrule or undermine analytics governance.
- The CEO and executive team take an active interest in (and perhaps participate in) analytics governance.
- Governance committees have visibility into analytics activities across the enterprise. They're not taken by surprise.
- Issues are resolved expeditiously at the appropriate level. The overall steering committee doesn't have to ask why everything gets referred all the way up.
- Resource providers—including IT staff responsible for data, user tools, and infrastructure—are committed to enabling analytics.
- Other governing bodies aren't questioning or second-guessing what analytics governance is up to.
- The governance model and charter evolve and "stay alive" as the enterprise succeeds through analytics and advances its analytical maturity.

We hope this discussion enables you and your organization to establish or refine your approach to governing your business analytics capabilities and initiatives. More importantly, we hope that effective governance enables you to amplify and accelerate the business results from analytics.

14

Building a Global Analytical Capability

Thomas H. Davenport

Analytics are being used successfully by companies around the globe to reduce risk, uncover new growth opportunities, and make existing business lines more efficient and profitable. Although the use of analytics is expanding, in most multinational companies there is little coordination of the organization's analytical initiatives. Substantial geographic variation in analytical approaches occurs within the same company. Some impressive analytical work takes place at corporate headquarters, and little goes on outside the home country—and sometimes vice versa. Teams typically operate independently within countries, business units, and functional areas, based on local conditions and requirements.

Based on conversations with analytics leaders around the world, few organizations are managing analytics globally. One reason is that not many organizations have anyone in charge of analytics at the global level. Rarely does a "Chief Analytics Officer" oversee analytical activity at a global level across all groups. More common is for different business units, functions, or country-based organizations to have their own analytics capabilities. Sometimes even within a country, siloed analytical groups can exist within functions or business units.

Widespread Geographic Variation

Even strong analytical competitors can have substantial geographic variation. Some examples may be useful. Take Tesco, for example. Based in the U.K., it's the world's third-largest retailer and has operations in 13 other countries. With the help of consultants dunnhumby (in which Tesco eventually bought a majority ownership share), the company pioneered the use of its loyalty card (ClubCard) data to target promotions to members. It's been a fantastically successful program. It is responsible in large part for Tesco's doubling its U.K. market share since Clubcard was introduced in 1995.[1]

However, there seems to be wide variation across countries in whether ClubCard—or an equivalent program—is offered and the extent to which its data is used to target promotions. It's definitely not offered in the company's U.S. Fresh & Easy chain, where loyalty programs are even somewhat disparaged on the website.[2] Korea—where Tesco operates a number of superstores (initially in a joint venture with Samsung, but now wholly owned) under the Homeplus brand—uses both a loyalty card (Familycard) and the resulting data.

Another example of geographic variation is Banco Santander, the Spain-based bank that is now the world's eighth largest in terms of assets. In Spain, there is a substantial focus on analytics, although the bank is not the market leader in that regard. In Brazil, Santander does not have a major focus on credit card analytics. Mexico, on the other hand, is quite aggressive on credit card analytics, basically emulating the very successful (in the U.S., at least) approaches of Capital One. In Germany, Santander has made major strides on credit scoring and automated loan decision models. However, at Sovereign Bank, the U.S. bank that Santander owns, there is little focus on analytics. The only global approach to analytics involves risk management, a consistent approach to which is somewhat mandated by Basel II regulations.

Is this geographic variation good or bad? One could argue that it's somewhat necessary given that regulations and available information vary across the world. In Brazil, for example, there is no such thing as a credit score (only binary indications of whether a particular customer is worthy of credit), which limits the ability to make loans on that basis. A head of analytics at a bank commented that the inability to get the same types of data globally was the greatest impediment to a common global analytics strategy.

But there is an opportunity to do more to standardize analytical approaches. Tesco, for example, is beginning to try to create more consistency and aggressive use of analytics through its dunnhumby subsidiary. The company has appointed an "Analytical Ambassador" to spread analytics through global subsidiaries.

Global Coordination of Analytics

Tesco's ambassador, however, is only the beginning of what can be undertaken in the realm of global coordination. Some other leading firms have taken a much more closely managed approach to coordinating analytical approaches around the globe. There are at least three possible global structure options:

- Central coordination through a common global analytics organization
- A strong *center of excellence* model that doesn't own all analytical groups but attempts to coordinate their efforts
- A *division of labor* model in which different groups around the globe specialize in particular analytical approaches

The following sections describe each of these global coordination models and provide examples.

Central Coordination, Centralized Organization

The most aggressive approach to global coordination of analytical activity is a central corporate organization to support analytics. Like all centralized structures, it allows for efficient, common approaches to solving business problems. Analysts in remote areas far from headquarters can still have been recruited, trained, and supervised from a central analytics organization—even if they also have local reporting relationships.

Of course, central organizations also have a downside. Analytical problems that can't be solved through common approaches may not get much focus. They may go unsolved or may require help from external consultants. The emphasis is on repeatable, standard solutions that can be solved through consistent models and software.

Procter & Gamble provides a good illustration of a centralized global coordination model. Several years ago, the corporate IT organization began to build and consolidate analytical people and renamed itself Information and Decision Solutions (IDS). Analytics were made a part of the Business Intelligence organization within IDS. A central group of analysts (divided into Commercial and Product Supply subgroups) at headquarters can work on a variety of solutions to be applied throughout P&G.

There are also analysts from IDS who support particular brands and geographic business units. The Asia business, for example, has someone responsible for business intelligence and analytics. The local analysts typically have close relationships with the leaders of individual business units and work on problems that the leaders have prioritized.

Using this central approach, P&G has rolled out a new approach to managing the business globally. It consists of more than 50 Business Spheres—special rooms designed for the display and discussion of business performance information and analyses. The information and analyses displayed are contained in a series of Business Sufficiency Models defined at headquarters, which continually evolve with new analyses and business challenges. It is unlikely that P&G could have developed and rolled out such a global approach without the global organization that supports it. Of course, the success of such an initiative also requires strong support from senior management, and CEO Bob McDonald has been a strong partner of IDS in the initiative.

A Strong Center of Excellence

A somewhat less centralized, but still effective, organizational model for global coordination requires the creation of a strong center of excellence to build and coordinate analytical activity. The actual center typically is composed of only a few people, and not all analysts report to them. But they have been deputized to take steps to build and acquire people with the necessary analytical skills, develop or subsidize the development of analytical solutions, and create structures for capturing and sharing analytical knowledge. Typically a head of analytics is at the top of the center, and there may be regional or unit-specific analytics heads as well.

This is a less centrally structured organization than the first one described, but it does require a substantial commitment to analytics. A firm couldn't establish all the necessary structures and positions in a center of excellence if it didn't believe that analytics were critical to its success. But compared to the fully centralized model, it does allow for greater focus on the idiosyncratic analytical problems of business units, geographies, and business functions that may be far from headquarters priorities. It also provides a structure for sharing analytical solutions and assets.

Perhaps the best examples of this approach come from professional services firms, several of which have established global initiatives and centers of excellence. Both Deloitte and Accenture, for example, have established global organizations to drive and support the development of analytical capabilities and the successful implementation of client projects. Deloitte, for example, has a global head of analytics (based in Singapore, but traveling widely) with a small staff. There are also heads of analytics in the Americas, Europe/Middle East/Africa, and Asia. In addition to these geographic organizations, there are also analytics groups with heads for particular practices (Audit, Tax, Consulting, Financial Advisory) and analytical domains (human capital, customer relationships, pricing, supply chain).

Although each group has considerable autonomy, annual global meetings are held to share ideas and solutions and report progress. An individual analytics practitioner may look to a variety of groups—only one of which involves analytics—for career direction and performance monitoring. However, this type of organization has allowed both Deloitte and Accenture—and several other firms as well—to quickly build analytical capabilities to serve external client needs.

A Coordinated "Division of Labor" Approach

Both of the organizational structures for global coordination just discussed require a high level of commitment to analytics and the devotion of considerable resources to building the organization. However, companies that don't have as much management commitment can employ a third approach that involves some coordination but less formal structure. It is a largely decentralized approach that also involves a small degree of coordination and collaboration through a recognized division of analytical expertise and labor. Analysts primarily work on local problems but devote a fraction of their time to developing solutions that can be spread across the company.

For example, one global insurance leader has developed a unique model over the past five years in its non-U.S. business that has leveraged local successes across the entire organization. Decentralized analysts in "data labs" across the world spend the bulk of their time focused on applying analytics to drive the business in their local market. But these analysts spend 10% to 15% of their time identifying best practices that could be leveraged on a global basis. A global center of excellence (consisting of only a global analytics leader and one other analyst) based in Hong Kong compiles the learnings from these disparate data labs, packages them, and disseminates them. In this way, this insurance provider has locally focused analysts but has developed an integrated global analytics capability. This effort has proven to senior leadership in the global business not only that analytics produces a positive ROI, but also that it is now a durable, global competitive advantage for the company.

The global business for this insurer is a $2 billion business that sells four insurance product lines in 27 countries. This business often works with affiliate partners and uses about 6,500 telemarketers to sell its products globally. Its U.S. business, where headquarters is located, focuses primarily on one line of insurance products and has a centralized analytics group of almost 50 people. However, the U.S. analytics function has no responsibilities outside that country and coordinates only with the global analytics group informally.

The company began competing on analytics in 2005. Initial efforts focused on using data to more effectively manage customer relationships. Soon, the focus evolved much more toward increasing overall customer value. As the effort matured, *customer value management* (CVM) was chosen as the name of the non-U.S. group. Although subtle, this choice of name connoted in the minds of senior management a business function rather than a simple application of technology. The formal definition of CVM is "the art and science of measuring, analyzing, and managing customer value." For this company, CVM is about testing, measuring, managing, and analyzing data to increase customer value (for both the company and its partners) while driving increased satisfaction for the end customer. In 2007, the insurance provider began working with affiliate partners in using intelligence generated from CVM to help these partners increase sales and commissions—work that continued through 2008 and 2009. The use of CVM has now extended across all of the company's product lines. The company has used CVM to help win new business and as part of new-product launches.

A CVM Center of Excellence (CoE) was established in Hong Kong in 2010. This small centralized organization has the resources and capacity to define and disseminate global CVM best practices. At the same time, this insurance provider has established "country data labs" in countries across the world. On average these labs have about three analysts who spend about 85% to 90% of their time focused on using analytics and CVM in their local market. They spend the remaining 10% to 15% of their time focused on establishing global best practices that can be used by other analysts at the company in other countries outside the U.S. (or theoretically in the U.S. too).

In addition to their day-to-day responsibilities working with local affinity partners, the labs in each market have a particular area of analytical concentration. For example, the lab in Taiwan concentrates on randomized testing and learning. In China the data lab is focused on product optimization. In Spain, which is the company's first market for a new private medical insurance (PMI) product, the data lab focuses on analyzing PMI. The learnings from each data lab are shared with the CoE in Hong Kong, which distills the findings and packages the key insights with the labs around the globe.

Now, five years into this journey, the CVM team can show positive returns. This insurer's global capabilities provide a competitive advantage against strong local competitors in each market. These global analytical capabilities are attractive to the company's partners because the capabilities provide insights that help improve commissions. The company's partners have experienced positive returns from the company's CVM capabilities, and they view CVM as a major differentiator. The use of analytics to build models results in better targeting of sales and marketing activities. Management strongly supports the CVM team, and the CVM analysts have unfettered access to whatever data they need to do their jobs.

Other Global Analytics Trends

In addition to these organizational structures for global coordination, I've abstracted a number of observations from travels and discussions with analysts and senior managers around the world:

- **Analytics lags ERP implementation.** In general, about five years after a firm implements an ERP system, it realizes it has a great deal of unused data, and some executive asks, "Weren't we supposed to do something with this data to better manage the business?" This leads to increased interest in analytics to leverage the data. One executive from SAS noted that this trend applies at the country level as well. About five years after the country's large organizations have completed ERP implementation, the business of analytics companies such as SAS picks up dramatically.

- **Financial services companies are the most active users of analytics.** Although there are analytical competitors in virtually all industries, the use of analytics in financial services is probably greatest around the world. In the wake of the financial crisis, it seems that financial companies are using analytics to help identify and manage their risks. Telecom, health care, and retail are other industries where analytics is beginning to take off around the globe. Governments are also developing a much stronger interest in analytics.

- **Analytics is being used to reduce risk and pursue new opportunities with customers.** Whether the primary use is risk reduction or pursuit of customer opportunity depends on the industry and the geography. In general, in Europe analytics are being used to mitigate risk and prevent customer attrition. In fast-growing economies in Asia, particularly in China, analytics are being used to capitalize on opportunities, and there is somewhat less interest in risk-oriented applications.

- **Data privacy is a growing issue everywhere.** Analysts and executives are concerned about data privacy and security in every region and country. They feel there is considerable uncertainty about how to deal with existing regulations, which vary widely across countries and even states within some countries. This uncertainty could affect the data that is available to analysts and how this data can be used. In addition, data privacy laws can change quickly, requiring that analysts and executives closely follow and stay abreast of these laws.

- **American advantages.** The United States has the most analytical competitors, perhaps because far more data is available in the U.S. for analysts to use. However, the lack of data in other geographies leads analysts to be creative and resourceful. The move to big data is also more pronounced in the U.S. than in other countries, although some Asian countries, including Singapore and South Korea, are displaying considerable interest in big-data analytics.

- **Recruiting analysts globally.** Other than in centrally managed analytics organizations such as Procter & Gamble (which regularly moves analysts through positions around the world), most labor markets for quantitative analysts are local. But finding people who can use data to tell compelling stories is quite difficult in every market. The approach at the insurance company described earlier has been to hire people with good analytical skills and then teach them about the business and how to use data to make a difference in the business.

- **Country-based investments in analytics and big data.** Over the last several years, we've begun to see countries that view analytics as key to their future economic development. Ireland, Singapore, and (very recently) the United States are examples of this trend. Analytics make sense as a growth area for Singapore for several reasons. Some of the country's previous growth domains, such as information technology manufacturing, have become somewhat commoditized. Singapore has scored high (first or third) in every TIMSS (Trends in International Mathematics and Science Study) ranking of mathematics achievement since 1995. Many Singaporeans speak excellent English—the language most often used to discuss analytics in business. Singapore has a strong industry foundation in financial services, one of the most analytical industries. Finally, the country's citizens are early and aggressive adopters of consumer technologies, which generate a lot of data for analysis. The government of Singapore has provided support for both university and private-sector programs. The Living Analytics

Research Centre[3] at Singapore Management University "seeks to make Singapore one of the world's premier locations for the development and applied use of real-time consumer and social analytics." The government also has funded other universities in areas involving big-data analytics. Furthermore, it supported the creation of the Deloitte Analytics Research Center in Singapore. In short, Singapore has decided that analytics are of sufficient promise as a driver of the nation's future economic growth that it is subsidizing a substantial research program on the topic. The Irish and U.S. governments have announced similar programs of research and education support, but on a smaller scale than Singapore.

Overall, we are still in the early days of global coordination and management of analytics programs. We are certain to see new approaches, and new examples of the models described in this chapter, as firms become more advanced and sophisticated in their use of analytics. The trend, however, is toward more coordination and collaboration over time, rather than less.

Endnotes

1. For more on the operation and history of Clubcard, see http://en.wikipedia.org/wiki/Tesco_Clubcard.

2. www.freshandeasy.com/WhoWeAre.aspx.

3. www.larc.smu.edu.sg/index.htm.

Part V
Case Studies in the Use of Analytics

15

Partners HealthCare System

Thomas H. Davenport

Partners HealthCare System was in 2012 the single largest provider of health care in the Boston area. It consisted of 12 hospitals with over 7,000 affiliated physicians. It had 4 million outpatient visits and 160,000 inpatient admissions a year. Partners was a nonprofit organization with almost $8 billion in revenues, and it spent over $1 billion per year on biomedical research. It was a major teaching affiliate of Harvard Medical School.

Partners was known as a "system," but it maintained substantial autonomy at each of its member hospitals. Although some information systems (the outpatient electronic medical record, for example) were standardized across Partners, other systems and data, such as patient scheduling, were specific to particular hospitals. Analytical activities also took place at both the centralized Partners level and individual hospitals such as Massachusetts General Hospital (MGH) and Brigham & Women's Hospital (usually called "the Brigham"). This chapter describes both centralized and hospital-specific analytical resources. The focus for hospital-specific analytics is the two major teaching hospitals of Partners—MGH and the Brigham—although other Partners hospitals also have their own analytical capabilities and systems.

Centralized Data and Systems at Partners

The basis of any hospital's clinical information systems is the clinical data repository, which contains information on all patients, their conditions, and the treatments they have received. The inpatient clinical data repository for Partners was initially implemented at the Brigham during the 1980s. Richard Nesson, the Brigham and Women's CEO, and John Glaser, the hospital's Chief Information Officer, initiated an outpatient electronic medical record (EMR) at the Brigham in 1989.[1] This EMR contributed outpatient data to the clinical data repository. The hospital was one of the first to embark upon an EMR, although MGH had begun to develop one of the first full-function EMRs as early as 1976.

A clinical data repository provides basic data about patients. Glaser and Nesson came to agree that in addition to a repository and an outpatient EMR, the Brigham—and Partners after 1994, when Glaser became its first CIO—needed facilities for doctors to input online orders for drugs, tests, and other treatments. Online ordering (called CPOE, or Computerized Provider Order Entry) would solve the time-honored problem of interpreting poor physician handwriting. If endowed with a bit of intelligence, CPOE also could check whether a particular order made sense for a particular patient. Did a prescribed drug comply with best-known medical practices? Did the patient have any adverse reactions to it in the past? Had the same test been prescribed six times before with no apparent benefit? Was the specialist to whom the patient was being referred covered by her health plan? With this type of medical and administrative knowledge built into the system, dangerous and time-consuming errors could be prevented. The Brigham embarked upon its CPOE system in 1989.

Nesson and Glaser knew that there were approaches other than CPOE to reducing medical errors. Some provider institutions, such as InterMountain Health Care in Utah, were focused on close adherence by physicians to well-established medical protocols. Others, like Kaiser Permanente in California and the Cleveland Clinic, combined insurance and medical practices in ways that incented all providers to work jointly on behalf of patients. Nesson and Glaser admired those approaches but felt that their impact would be less in an academic medical center such as Partners, where physicians were somewhat autonomous, and departments prided themselves on their individual reputations for research and practice innovations. Common, intelligent systems seemed like the best way to improve patient care at Partners.

In 1994, when the Brigham and Mass General combined as Partners HealthCare System, there was still considerable autonomy for individual hospitals in the combined organization. However, from the onset of the merger, the two hospitals agreed to use a common outpatient EMR called the longitudinal medical record (LMR) and a CPOE system, both of which were developed at the Brigham. This was powerful testimony in favor of the LMR and CPOE systems because there was considerable rivalry between the two hospitals, and Mass General had its own EMR.

Perhaps the greatest challenge was educating the extended network of Partners-affiliated physicians about the LMR and CPOE. The physician network of over 6,000 practicing generalist and specialist physician groups was scattered around the Boston metropolitan area and often operated out of their own private offices. Many lacked the IT or telecom infrastructures to implement the systems on their own, and implementation of an outpatient EMR cost about $25,000 per physician. Yet full use of the system across Partners-affiliated providers was critical to a seamless patient experience across the organization.

Glaser and the Partners Information Systems (IS) organization worked diligently to spread the LMR and CPOE to the growing number of Partners hospitals and to Partners-affiliated physicians and medical practices. To assist in bringing physicians outside the hospitals on board, Partners negotiated payment schedules with insurance companies that rewarded physicians for supplying the kind of information available from the LMR and CPOE. By 2007, 90% of Partners-affiliated physicians were using the systems, and by 2009, 100% were. By 2009, over 1,000 orders per hour were being entered through the CPOE system across Partners.

The combination of the LMR and CPOE proved to be a powerful one in helping avoid medical errors. *Adverse drug events*—the use of the wrong drug for a condition or a drug that caused an allergic reaction—typically were encountered by about 14 of every 1,000 inpatients across the U.S. At the Brigham before the LMR and CPOE, the number was about 11. After the widespread implementation of these systems at Brigham and Women's, a little more than five adverse drug events occurred per 1,000 inpatients—a 55% reduction.

In 2012 Partners announced that it was considering replacing its homegrown EMR system with one from Epic Systems Corp. The move was driven in part by Dr. David Blumenthal, who was named the first national coordinator for health information technology under the Obama administration. Blumenthal returned to Partners in 2011 as chief health information and innovation officer—the first person to hold such a role. He commented in a news story on the disparate systems at Partners that led the organization to consider a commercial EMR:

> "The result is, when patients move from one place to another, their information often does not follow them in a complete form or as promptly as we'd like," said Dr. David Blumenthal, Partners chief health information and innovation officer. Under the new system, data for a patient who is referred from a primary care office to an orthopedist, has surgery, and later is discharged with home care would be contained "all in the same record and all available in real time," he said. The change would make it easier to update the system as the technology evolves and to apply quality control tools—such as prompts about appropriate tests or warnings of possible drug interactions—uniformly across all Partners practices, Blumenthal said.[2]

Managing Clinical Informatics and Knowledge at Partners

The Clinical Informatics Research and Development (CIRD) group, headed by Blackford Middleton, was one of the key centralized resources for health care analytics at Partners. Many of CIRD's staff, like Middleton, had multiple advanced degrees. Middleton had an MD, a Master of Public Health degree, and a Master of Science in Health Services Research. CIRD's mission was

> ...to improve the quality and efficiency of care for patients at Partners HealthCare System by assuring that the most advanced current knowledge about medical informatics

(clinical computing) is incorporated into clinical information systems at Partners HealthCare.[3]

CIRD was part of the Partners IS organization.

It was CIRD's role to help create the strategy for how Partners used information systems in patient care, and to develop production systems capabilities and pilot projects that employ informatics and analytics. CIRD's work had played a substantial role in making Partners a worldwide leader in the use of data, analysis, and computerized knowledge to improve patient care. CIRD also had several projects funded by U.S. government health agencies to adapt some of the same tools and approaches it developed for Partners to the broader health care system.

One key function of CIRD was to manage clinical knowledge and translate health care research findings into daily medical practice at Partners. In addition to facilitating adoption of the LMR and CPOE, Partners faced a major challenge in getting control of the clinical knowledge that was made available to care providers through these and other systems. The "intelligent CPOE" strategy demanded that knowledge be online, accessible, and easily updated so that it could be referenced by and presented to care providers in real-time interactions with patients. Of course, a variety of other online knowledge tools, such as medical literature searching, were available to Partners personnel; in total they were referred to as the Partners Handbook. At one point after use of the CPOE had become widespread at Brigham and Women's, a comparison was made between online usage of the Handbook and usage of the knowledge base from order entry. There were more than 13,000 daily accesses through the CPOE system at the Brigham alone, and only 3,000 daily accesses of the Handbook by all Partners personnel at all hospitals. Therefore, there was an ongoing effort to ensure that as much high-quality knowledge as possible made it into the CPOE.

The problem with knowledge at Partners wasn't that there wasn't enough of it; indeed, the various hospitals, labs, departments, and individuals were overflowing with knowledge. The problem was how to manage it. At one point, Tonya Hongsermeier, a physician with an MBA degree who was charged with managing knowledge at Partners, counted the number of places around Partners where some form of rules-based knowledge about clinical practice was not centrally managed. She found about 23,000 of them. The knowledge was contained in a variety of formats: paper documents, computer screen shots, process flow diagrams, references, and data or reports on clinical outcomes—all in a variety of locations, and only rarely shared.

Hongsermeier set out to create a "knowledge engineering and management" factory that would capture the knowledge at Partners, put it in a common format and central repository, and make it available for CPOE and other online systems. This required not only a new computer system for holding the thousands of rules that constituted the knowledge, but an extensive human system for gathering, certifying, and maintaining the knowledge. It consisted of the following roles and organizations:

- A set of committees of senior physicians who oversaw clinical practice in various areas, such as the Partners Drug Therapy Committee, that reviewed and sanctioned the knowledge as correct or best-known practice
- A group of subject matter experts who, using online collaboration systems, debated and refined knowledge such as the best drug for treating high cholesterol under various conditions, or the best treatment protocol for diabetes patients
- A cadre of "knowledge editors" who took the approved knowledge from these groups and put it into a rules-based form that would be accepted by the online knowledge repository

High-Performance Medicine at Partners

Glaser and Partners IS had always had the support of senior Partners executives. But for the most part their involvement in the activities designed to build Partners' informatics and analytics capabilities was limited to some of the hospitals and physician practices that wanted to be on the leading edge. Then Jim Mongan moved from being President of MGH (a role he had occupied since 1996, shortly after the creation of Partners) to being CEO of Partners overall in January 2003. Not since Dick Nesson had Glaser had such a strong partner in the executive suite.

Mongan had come to appreciate the value of the LMR and CPOE, and other clinical systems, while he headed Mass General. But when he came into the Partners CEO role, with responsibility for a variety of diverse and autonomous institutions, he began to view it differently.

> So when I was preparing to make the move to Partners, I began to think about what makes a health system. One of the keys that would unite us was the electronic record. I saw it as the connective tissue, the thing we had in common, that could help us get a handle on utilization, quality, and other issues.[4]

Together Mongan and Glaser agreed that although Partners already had strong clinical systems and knowledge management compared to other institutions, a number of weaknesses still needed to be addressed (most importantly, that the systems were not universally used across Partners care settings). Steps needed to be taken to get to the next level of capability. Working with other clinical leaders at Partners, they began to flesh out the vision for what came to be known as the High-Performance Medicine (HPM) initiative, which took place between 2003 and 2009.

Glaser commented on the process the team followed to specify the details of the HPM initiative:

> Shortly after he took the reins at Partners, however, Jim had a clear idea on where he wanted this to go. To help refine that vision, several of us went on a road trip, to learn from other highly integrated health systems such as Kaiser, Intermountain Health Care, and the Veterans Administration about ways we might bring the components of our system closer together.

Mongan concluded:

> We also were working with a core team of 15 to 20 clinical leaders and eventually came up with a list of seven or eight initiatives, which then needed to be prioritized. We did a *Survivor*-style voting process to determine which initiatives to "kick off the island." That narrowed down the list to five Signature Initiatives.

The five initiatives consisted of the following specific programs, each of which was addressed by its own team:

- **Creating an IT infrastructure.** Much of the initial work of this program had already been done. It consisted of the LMR and CPOE, which was extended to the other hospitals and physician practices in the Partners network and maintained. This project also addressed patient data quality reporting, further enhancement of knowledge management processes, and a patient data portal to give patients access to their own health information.

- **Enhancing patient safety.** The team addressing patient safety issues focused on four specific projects:
  - Providing decision support about what medications to administer in several key areas, including renal and geriatric dosing
  - Communicating "clinically significant test results," particularly to physicians after their patients have left the hospital
  - Ensuring effective flow of information during patient care transitions and handoffs in hospitals and after discharge
  - Providing better decision support, patient education, best practices, and metrics for anticoagulation management

- **Uniform high quality.** This team addressed quality improvement in the specific domains of hospital-based cardiac care, pneumonia, diabetes care, and smoking cessation. It employed both registries and decision support tools to do so. This team also took the lead in incorporating aspects of the SmartForms project into the LMR and CPOE systems.

- **Chronic disease management.** The team addressing disease management focused on preventing hospital admissions by identifying Partners patients who were at highest risk for hospitalization. Then they developed health coaching programs to address patients with high levels of need, such as heart failure patients. The team also pulled together a new database of information about patient wishes concerning end-of-life decisions.

- **Clinical resource management.** At Mongan's suggestion, the team focused on how to lower the usage of high-cost drugs and high-cost imaging services. It employed both "low-tech" methods (such as chart reviews) and "high-tech" approaches (such as a data warehouse making transparent physician's imaging behaviors relative to peers) to begin making use of scarce resources more efficient.

Overall, Partners spent about $100 million on HPM and related clinical systems initiatives, most of which were ultimately paid for by the Partners hospitals and physician practices that used them. To track progress, a Partners-wide report, called the HPM Close, was developed that shows current and trend performance on the achievement of quality, efficiency, and structural goals. The report was published quarterly to ensure timely feedback for measuring performance and supporting accountability across Partners.

New Analytical Challenges for Partners

Partners had made substantial progress on many of the basic approaches to clinical analytics, but there were many other areas at the intersection of health and analytics that it could still address. One was the area of "personalized genetic medicine"—the idea that patients would someday receive specific therapies based on their genomic, proteomic, and metabolic information. Partners had created i2b2 (Informatics for Integrating Biology and the Bedside), a "National Center for Biomedical Computing," that was funded by the National Institutes of Health. Glaser was codirector of i2b2 and developed the IT infrastructure for the Partners Center for Personalized Genetic Medicine. One of the many issues these efforts addressed in personalized genetic medicine was how relevant genetic information would be included in the LMR.

Partners was also attempting to use clinical information for "post-market surveillance"—identifying problems with drugs and medical devices after they have been released to the market. Some Partners researchers had identified dangerous side effects from certain drugs through analysis of LMR data. Specifically, Research Scientist John Brownstein's analyses suggested that the baseline expected level of heart attack admissions to Mass General and the Brigham had increased 18 percent beginning in 2001 and returned to its baseline level in 2004. This increase coincided with the time frame for the beginning and end of Vioxx prescriptions. Thus far the identification of problems had taken place only after researchers from other institutions had identified them, but Partners executives believed they could identify the problems at an earlier stage. The institution collaborated with the Food and Drug Administration and the Department of Defense to accelerate the surveillance process. Glaser noted:

> I don't know that we'll get as much specificity as might be needed to really challenge whether a drug ought to be in a market, but I also think it's fairly clear that you can be much faster and involve much fewer funds, frankly, to do what we would call the "canary in the mine" approach.[5]

Partners was also focused on the use of communications technologies to improve patient care. Its Center for Connected Health, headed by Dr. Joe Kvedar, developed one of the first physician-to-physician online consultation services in an academic medical setting. The Center also explored combinations of remote monitoring technologies, sensors (for example, pill boxes that know whether today's dosage has been taken), and online communications and intelligence to improve patient adherence to medication regimes, engagement in personal health, and clinical outcomes.

In the clinical knowledge management area, Partners had done an impressive job of organizing and maintaining the many rules and knowledge bases that informed its "intelligent" CPOE system. However, it was apparent to Glaser, Blackford Middleton, and Tonya Hongsermeier—and her successor as head of knowledge management, Roberto Rocha—that it made little sense for each medical institution to develop its own knowledge base. Therefore, Partners was actively engaged in helping other institutions manage clinical knowledge. Middleton (the principal investigator), Hongsermeier, Rocha, and at least 13 other Partners employees were involved in a major Clinical Decision Support Consortium project funded by the U.S. Agency for Healthcare Research and Quality. The consortium involved a variety of other research institutions and health care companies. It focused primarily on finding ways to make clinical knowledge widely available to health care providers through EMR and CPOE systems furnished by leading vendors.

Despite all these advances, not all Partners executives and physicians had fully bought into the vision of using smart information systems to improve patient care. For example, some believed the LMR and CPOE were invasive in the relationship between doctor and patient. A senior cardiologist at Brigham and Women's, for example, stated the following in an interview:

> I have a problem with the algorithmic approach to medicine. People end up making rote decisions that don't fit the patient, and it can also be medically quite wasteful. I don't have any choice here if I want to write prescriptions—virtually all of them are done online. But I must say that I am getting alert fatigue. Every time I write a prescription for nitroglycerine, I am given an alert that asks me to ensure that my patient isn't on Viagra. Don't you think I know that at this point? As for online treatment guidelines, I believe in them up to a point. But once something is in computerized guidelines it's sacrosanct, whether or not the data are legitimate. Recommendations should be given with notification of how certain we are about them.... Maybe these things are more useful to some doctors than others. If you're in a subspecialty like cardiology, you know it very well. But if you are an internist, you may have shallow knowledge, because you have to cover a wide variety of medical issues.

Many of the people involved in developing computer systems for patient care at Partners regarded these as valid concerns. "Alert fatigue," for example, had been recognized as a problem within Middleton's group for several years. They had tried to eliminate the more obvious alerts and make changes in the system to allow physicians to modify the types of alerts they received. There was a difficult line to draw, however, between keeping physician attention and saving lives.

Centralized Business Analytics at Partners

Much of the centralized analytical activity at Partners had been on the clinical side, but the organization also was making progress on business analytics. The primary focus of these efforts was financial reporting and analysis.

For several years, for example, Partners employed an external "software as a service" tool to provide reporting on the organization's revenue cycle. It had also developed several customized analytics applications in the areas of cash management, underpayments, bad debt reserves, and charge capture. These activities took place primarily in the Partners Revenue Finance function.

The Partners Information Systems organization was also increasing its focus on administrative and financial analytics. It was putting in place Compass, a common billing and administrative system, at all Partners hospitals. At the same time, Partners had created a set of standard processes for collecting, defining, and modifying financial and administrative data. Furthermore, as one article put it:

> At Partners, John Stone, corporate director for financial and administrative systems, is developing a corporate center of business analytics and business intelligence. Some 12 to 14 financial executives will oversee the center, define Partners' strategy for data management, and determine data-related budget priorities. "Our analysts spend the majority of their time gathering, cleaning, and scrubbing administrative data and less time providing value-added analytics and insight into what the data is saying," says Stone. "We want to flip that equation so our analysts are spending more time producing a story that goes along with the data."[6]

Hospital-Specific Analytical Activities: Massachusetts General Hospital

MGH, because it was a highly research-driven institution, had long focused primarily on clinical research and the resulting clinical informatics and analytics. In addition to the LMR and CPOE systems used by Partners overall, MGH researchers and staff had developed a number of IT tools to analyze and search clinical data, including a tool that searched across multiple enterprise clinical systems, including the LMR.

Historically, the research, clinical, information systems, and analytics-focused business arms of MGH tended to operate in narrow and rigidly defined roles. However, the challenges of an evolving health care landscape forced a change in that paradigm. For instance, a strong focus at MGH in 2011 was on how to achieve federal "meaningful-use" reimbursement for the organization's expenditures on EMR. Because achieving meaningful-use objectives is predicated on a high level of coordination among information systems, the physicians and business intelligence people were beginning to collaborate extensively. These were people like David Y. Ting, the Associate Medical Director for *Information Systems* for *MGH* and Massachusetts General Physicians Organization, and Chris Hutchins, Director of Finance Systems and Deputy CIO.

The HITECH/ARRA criteria for Stage 1 EMR meaningful use prescribed 25 specific objectives to give providers incentives to adopt and use electronic health records.[7] The incentive from the federal government is up to $44,000 for each eligible provider who fulfilled the meaningful-use criteria. MGH had examined the objectives and broken them into ten major pieces of patient data that physicians need to record in the EMR. However, many are not relevant for all its physicians. For example, a primary care physician would logically enter such data as demographics, vital signs, and smoking status, but these would be less relevant for certain specialists to enter.

In order to raise the level of EMR use by all its providers, as well as to provide resources for the work needed to achieve that level, MGH arrived at a novel funds distribution model. They determined that the physicians organization would reserve a portion of the pool of $44,000 per physician toward IT and analytics infrastructure. Then it would distribute the remaining incentive payment across all providers, proportional to the amount of data a particular physician is charged with entering. An internal quality incentive program would serve as the distribution mechanism. For example, if a physician recorded demographics, vital signs, and smoking status for the requisite number of patients, he would receive 30% of the per-physician payment from the pool. If he fulfilled all 10 quality measures, he would receive 100% of the payment. This encouraged all physicians to contribute to the meaningful-use program, but it also meant that no physicians would receive the full amount of $44,000.

Clearly, such a complex quality incentive model required an unprecedented level of analytics. Currently, Ting, Hutchins, and others at MGH are working to map the myriad clinical and finance data sources that are scattered among individual departments, exist at a hospital site level, or exist at the Partners enterprise level. Simultaneously, they must negotiate data governance agreements even among other Partners entities. This ensures that the requisite data feeds from sources within Partners and pertaining to MGH, but stored outside MGH's physical data warehouses, were available for MGH analytics purposes.

MGH has some experience with reimbursement metrics based on physician behaviors, having used them in Partners Community HealthCare, Inc. (PCHI), its physician network in the Boston area. PCHI has provided physician incentives on the basis of admission rates, cost-effective use of pharmacy and imaging services, and screening for particular diseases and conditions, such as diabetes. This was also the mechanism used to encourage physicians to adopt the LMR and CPOE systems. But MGH, like other providers, struggled with developing clear and transparent metrics across the institution that could help drive awareness and new behaviors. If MGH could create broadly accessible metrics on individual physicians' frequency of prescribing generic drugs, for example, it would undoubtedly drive MGH's competitive physicians to excel in the rankings.

On the business side, MGH was trying to develop a broad set of capabilities in business intelligence and analytics. A Business Intelligence/Performance Management group had recently been created under the direction of Chris Hutchins, Deputy CIO and Director of Finance Systems for the Mass General Physicians Organization. The group was generating reports on certain financial and administrative topics:

- Billing efficiency, claims adjudication, rejection rates, and times to resolve billing accounts, both at MGH overall and across practices
- Improving patient access, average wait times to see a physician, cancellation and no-show rates
- Employer attrition as an MGH customer

MGH was also working with the CMS (Centers for Medicare and Medicaid Services) on the Physician Quality Reporting Initiative. To combine all these measures in a meaningful fashion, the Massachusetts General Physicians Organization was also working on a balanced scorecard.[8] At the moment, however, Hutchins felt that the scorecard was still early in its development, so current efforts focused on identifying leading indicators.

Although the current analytical activity largely concerned reporting, Hutchins planned to develop more capabilities around alerts, exception reporting, and predictive models. The MGH Physicians Organization was implementing capabilities for statistical and predictive analytics that would be applied to several topics. For example, one key area in which better prediction would be useful involved patient volume. They were also pursuing more general models that would predict shifts in business over time.

Hospital-Specific Analytical Activities: Brigham & Women's Hospital

Like MGH, the Brigham's analytical activities in the past had been largely focused on clinical research. Now, however, it was also addressing much of the same business, operational, and meaningful-use issues as MGH. Many of the analytical activities at the Brigham were pursued by the Center for Clinical Excellence, which was founded by Dr. Michael Gustafson in 2001. The center had five functionally interrelated sections:

- Quality programs
- Patient safety
- Performance improvement
- Decision support systems (including all internal and external data management and reporting activities)
- Analysis and planning (which oversees business plan development, ROI assessments for major investments, cost benchmarking, asset utilization reporting, and support for strategic planning)

The CCE had close working relationships with the Brigham's CFO and Finance organizations, the Brigham's Information Systems organization, the Partners Business Development and Planning function, and other centers and medical departments at the Brigham.

One major difference between the Brigham and MGH (and most other hospitals, for that matter) was that the Brigham established a balanced scorecard beginning in 2000. It was based on a well-established cultural orientation to operational and quality metrics throughout the hospital. Richard Nesson, the Brigham CEO who had partnered with CIO John Glaser to introduce the LMR and CPOE systems, was also a strong advocate of information-driven decision-making on both the clinical and business sides of the hospital. The original systems that Nesson and Glaser had established also incorporated a reporting tool called EX and a data warehouse called CHASE (Computerized Hospital Analysis System for Efficiency). The analyses and data from these systems formed the core of the Brigham's balanced scorecard.

Before an effective scorecard could be developed, the Brigham had to undertake considerable work on data definitions and management. One analysis discovered, for example, that five different definitions of the length of a patient stay were circulating in 11 different reports. The Chief Medical Officer at the time, Dr. Andy Whittemore, and the CCE's Dr. Gustafson, a surgeon who had just taken on quality measurement issues at the Brigham, addressed these data issues with a senior executive steering committee. They decided to present the data in an easy-to-digest scorecard.

Under the ongoing management of the CCE, the scorecard contained a variety of financial, operational, and clinical metrics from across the hospital. The choice of metrics was driven by a "strategy map"[9] specifying the relationships between key variables that drove the hospital's performance (see Figure 15.1). Unlike most corporate strategy maps, financial performance variables were at the bottom of the map rather than the top. The hospital-wide scorecard had more than 50 specific measures, and departments such as Nursing and Surgery had more detailed scorecards. The scorecard also had been extended to Faulkner Hospital, a Partners institution that was managed jointly with Brigham.

Dr. Gary Gottlieb, the Brigham president from 1992 to 2009, was the most aggressive user of the scorecard. He noted the following:

I review the balanced scorecard on a regular basis because there is specific data that is of interest to me. There are key metrics I examine for trends and if they develop, then I analyze the data to better understand what is going right or wrong. It is one view, but an important one of our hospital. I can look at the balanced scorecard and get information in another way, from a different perspective than I can when I'm making rounds on a hospital unit, or sitting in the meeting with chiefs.

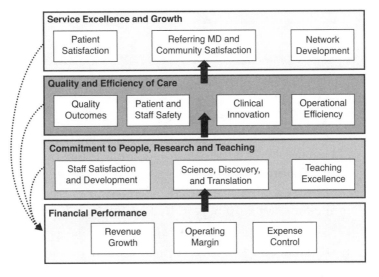

Figure 15.1 Strategy map for Brigham & Women's balanced scorecard.

Gottlieb left the Brigham CEO role to become the CEO of Partners overall in 2010. One of the primary initiatives in his new Partners role was to expand the degree of common systems throughout Partners so that there could be common data and analytics throughout the organization. Perhaps one day, he speculated, all of Partners Health-Care System would be managed through one scorecard.

Endnotes

1. This and other details of the Partners LMR/CPOE systems are derived from Richard Kesner, "Partners Healthcare System: Transforming Health Care Services Delivery Through Information Management," Ivey School of Business Case study, 2009.

2. Chelsea Conaboy, "Partners HealthCare in Talks to Buy New Electronic Records System," *Boston Globe*, May 17, 2012.

3. www.partners.org/cird/.

4. "HPM and IT: A Successful Working Partnership: Q&A with James Mongan and John Glaser," Partners IS Newsletter, Winter 2010, p. 1.

5. PricewaterhouseCoopers, "Partners HealthCare: Using EHR data for post-market surveillance of drugs," 2009.

6. Healthcare Financial Management Association, "Developing a Meaningful EHR," www.hfma.org/Publications/Leadership-Publication/Archives/Special-Reports/Spring-2010/Developing-a-Meaningful-EHR/, Part 3 of "Leadership Spring-Summer 2010 Report: Collaborating for Results."

7. The 25 meaningful-use criteria are described in www.healthcareitnews.com/news/eligible-provider-meaningful-use-criteria.

8. Kaplan, Robert S. and Norton, David P. "The Balanced Scorecard: Measures that Drive Performance," *Harvard Business Review*, January–February 1992.

9. Kaplan, Robert S. and Norton, David P. "Having Trouble With Your Strategy? Then Map It," *Harvard Business Review*, September–October 2000.

16

Analytics in the HR Function at Sears Holdings Corporation

Carl Schleyer

Three years ago in March of 2009, I was given the opportunity to build an HR Analytics team within the HR function of Sears Holdings Corporation (SHC). Strategic planning sessions had identified analytics as a specific gap in the services HR was providing. At the time, metrics from HR and Finance did not agree on basic things such as headcount or payroll. There were multiple legacy HR systems, and standards were not in place; for example, each business unit had its own way of calculating turnover. So building analytic capability was added as a core pillar to our internal HR mission statement.

The culture of data-driven decisions at SHC has helped drive demand for our services. Challenging economic conditions since 2008 have created a difficult environment for all retailers, and the merger of the Kmart and Sears companies left a good portion of our leadership team new in their roles. That created fertile ground for HR analytics because business leaders were open to new ideas and eager for better information about decision-making. Today, with a high degree of executive sponsorship, we almost never have to push our services on clients, but rather have the opposite problem—too much demand.

What We Do

Our team has a broad vision: To become the industry leader in HR analytics by supplying data-derived insights to HR, SHC, and business leaders—insights that enable strategic decision-making and optimize decisions about people. Anything of potential value is in scope. Our work includes classic elements of HR accountability:

- Building actionable HR scorecards based on metrics that are predictive of customer service and employee engagement
- Building strategic HR dashboards that track retention, career development, and leadership effectiveness
- Validating assessments and uncovering learning to influence new employee sourcing and selection
- Using analytics to strengthen the performance management system and design probationary periods
- Displaying the natural career paths of job groups and recommending ways to strengthen associate development—both through key "feeder" roles and by identifying business critical or pivotal jobs

But our work also includes people-related questions around staffing, scheduling, physical work environment, and department configurations.

We prioritize requests based on value creation, complexity, and business impact. This means we stay occupied with some pretty intensive analytic research and models, but we also sprinkle in small, quick wins as a way for analysts to relax their minds and take a break from the monster problems they've been tackling all week.

The phrase "Fresh-Squeezed Insights Served Daily" has become our team's motto for two reasons. First, the word "insight" serves as a constant reminder that, while the client may have asked for us to provide data, insights are what they really need. So even on the simple requests, we aim to provide context—comparison to last year, to comparable companies, external benchmarks, or what we know from academic research. Although that takes a bit more time, it greatly enhances usability of our work products. Second, the words "fresh" and "daily" are about our work being relevant to business problems right now. It encourages our key clients to leverage us frequently without feeling guilty about multiple requests in a week.

It's also important to understand what we don't work on—what we say "no" to. We have a rule of thumb that our time is worth $2,000 per hour. Although that is not what I pay my analysts or bill my clients, it is an estimate of the annual value we create for the organization. That rule governs everything from which meetings we attend and which projects we double up on, to how deep to go in the research, when to stop an effort, and most importantly, what projects don't make the priority list. For example, probing the attributes of successful specialized sales associates who specialize in water heaters is not as important to the organization as understanding the thousands of associates who sell appliances or electronics.

Saying "no" is an under-appreciated leadership skill; but if you want to keep precious resources focused on strategic, high-value problems, you've got to get good at it. Responses that redirect, such as "Here is some internal research we did on a similar topic" and "Data we publish monthly in the HR Scorecard will provide 90% of what you are looking for" are ways to say "no" without ever using the word. If the redirect doesn't work, another tactic is to zoom out and respond to a specific request with an enterprise or companywide solution. For example, if we receive a request for turnover trends of a job code, department, or business unit, with almost the same work investment, we can deliver a solution that answers the question for others across the company. Finally, refocusing the question by probing into what problem is trying to be solved or what the client is attempting to do helps ensure our work investment is productive.

Who Make Good HR Analysts

Don't be tricked into believing you need a lot of quant jocks or statistics PhDs. We staff our team with curious HR professionals. Industrial and organizational psychologists are particularly well-prepared for analyst roles like this because of their formal education with statistical tools and the scientific method. So are people with an Economics minor or undergraduate degree. Because of expansion and internal promotion, we've had to source for HR Analysts a number of times. I'm convinced that success depends on the following four competencies or types of intelligence:

1. Business Intelligence is really the most important attribute, essential to building relationships with operations or line management. This includes an understanding of important factors in the business environment, the ability to present and communicate findings and insights in an easy-to-understand way, and the desire to partner with the business to sharpen focus and implement change.

2. Analytical Intelligence is asking the right questions of the data and taking initiative to understand the "why" behind the "what." Here we are looking for strong ability to manipulate data to create insight. We look for curiosity in approaches to research and unique ways of squeezing value out of data.

3. Systems Intelligence refers to understanding general information systems, including how and where data is stored. People who have implemented, managed, or built HR software can quickly learn new programs. We also look for a demonstrated ability to get at data that others believed to be unavailable.

4. HR Intelligence resides in people who have figured out the human capital levers that drive top-line and bottom-line growth. It includes general knowledge of HR practices and regulations, plus the ability to communicate with other HR professionals in a credible manner.

Our interview process is built around these attributes. Asking questions like "When did examining outliers shape the course of a project?" helps us evaluate analytical intelligence as well as personal curiosity. Having candidates "Describe an interesting unintended consequence after you applied an intervention" helps us gauge human resource savvy as well as business acumen. Interviews conclude with a short case study, and the recommendations or solutions our candidates present point out the areas in which they are strongest and most comfortable. It is pretty rare to find one candidate who scores high in all four competencies, but staffing your team with diversity of strengths is a way to encourage collaboration and cross training.

Our everyday management practices are designed to build good analysts. The team is centrally located, which enables sharing of tips, building off prior experience, spontaneous brainstorming, and testing of hypotheses among like-minded peers. We also give analysts a lot of autonomy and the capacity to experiment. Some of our most valuable ideas have come from providing curious and creative analysts space to tackle their "wish lists." Nothing squashes creativity faster than an urgent deadline, so we endeavor to spread deliverables appropriately and provide slack in our "insight manufacturing system."

Our Recipe for Maximum Value

Although every project and question is unique, we began to notice our most successful work outputs contained the following components. When these ingredients are mixed together lovingly, your clients are guaranteed to come back for more!

- **25% Data.** Gather, clean, and connect disparate data. Use only the freshest data you can afford, and pay attention to what outliers can teach you about data quality. Partner with Finance or Operations to share work burden and create partnerships; you'll often work with those teams on your pursuit of rigorous data.

- **10% Stakeholders.** Collect key hypotheses from executives. This is a great way to "sift the lumps" out of your research questions. But keep the conversations brief so that they don't taint your ability to treat the data with an open mind. Create memorable flavor by sprinkling in a pinch of business myth-busting. (Caution: Too much can spoil productive collaboration.)

- **15% Analysis.** A few HR professionals will need to become familiar with advanced math, or you can "in-source" analysts from your customer, marketing, or strategy teams. (They tend to be willing to help the folks who manage pay and career opportunities.)

- **20% Storytelling.** Reduce the research stock into one memorable slide. Explain what the insights mean and how to take them into action. Shake financial acumen liberally into the story because no proposal is worth a leader's time unless it expresses itself in financial outcomes. Go as deep as you need to behind the scenes, but remember that the savory flavor of regression, T-tests, and P-values is an acquired taste for most.

- **20% Implementation.** Here is where the homemade flavor really stands out! Resistance or obstacles encountered likely point to shortcuts taken in stakeholding or the analysis. Involving HR analysts in the implementation enables them to gain the business intimacy that shapes future projects in actionable ways.

- **10% Embedding.** Top off your delicacy by defining accountabilities, embedding purposeful reporting, and transferring operational ownership. Celebrate short term wins. Set a specific date to monitor outcomes. And remain flexible—modify the business change plan if necessary.

Key Lessons Learned

My three years of dedicated focus on HR metrics, measurement, and analytics could be described as crawl, walk, and now run. When we got started, there wasn't much industry information about how to form a team, what work to do, or how to do it. So I jumped in head first, rolled up my sleeves, and learned some important lessons:

- **Behavior.** In the space between strategy and outcomes is human behavior. The secret to unlocking value has been to focus on behaviors that lead to outcomes rather than on measuring the outcomes alone. This is not an easy task because the outcome data (sales, turnover, customer service) is readily available, whereas the data required to build behavior metrics often does not yet exist. Galileo is my personal source of inspiration: "Measure what is measurable, and make measurable what is not so."

- **Momentum.** How many times have you been in a meeting that ended with the decision that "we need more data to make a decision?" A trick we use to help speed progress is asking "What would you do differently if you knew the answer to that question?" That helps us get underneath client concerns as well as politely surfacing the fact that enough information probably exists to make a decision.

- **Attention.** Learn to listen well. Your head has two ears and only one mouth. Using them in that proportion helps discover business pain points, what organizational hypotheses are in operation, and which myths are worth busting.

- **Purpose.** Be sure to balance the immediate with the important, and don't let what is urgent win over what's truly critical. This also applies to designing reports—every tool should answer a question. Don't be shy about putting the purpose statements right at the top to focus clients on how to interpret the information.

- **Action.** You may have worked hundreds of hours on a problem and are super-proud of your statistical models or data creativity. But when it comes to telling your story, remember that your client wants "less information and more application." Keep your executive recaps focused on insights that influence decisions and actions that drive value through change.

- **Partnership.** Partner heavily with Finance and Operations. Learn to speak their language and understand their pain points. It's always a proud moment when clients forget which functional team we work on and view us as performance improvement consultants.

- **Software.** Credibility comes from confidently knowing. Analytics need to go deeper than means and medians, so invest in good statistical software. We are quite fond of JMP, a statistical discovery product from SAS. The product's drag-and-drop interface makes it simple for HR professionals to learn. It's visual, highly interactive, and very cost effective.

- **Chartology.** Never underestimate the power of a good visual. If my twin 6–year-olds have taught me anything about attention span, it's that capturing someone's attention happens even before the first word is spoken. A good visual will combine "show" and "tell" to speed understanding.

These capabilities are helping the leadership of Sears Holdings close the strategy-execution gap while at the same time solving frontline worker retention, engagement, and career path issues. I am very thankful that my skills, abilities, and background merged at the perfect time as the HR profession becomes more analytical.

17

Commercial Analytics Culture and Relationships at Merck

Thomas H. Davenport

The Commercial Analytics and Decision Sciences group at Merck is responsible for assisting with advanced analytics for all of the U.S. primary care, hospital/specialty, and vaccine products at Merck. Its focus is sales and marketing analytics, including customer targeting, segmentation, sales force sizing, promotion response modeling, ROI assessments, and other related analyses. The group's primary mission is to help senior leaders at Merck make better business decisions about multimillion-dollar promotional and sales budgets. It has existed at Merck for over 15 years.

The group consists of over 25 full-time staff and several other external consultants. The leader of the group has a PhD in Applied Research and Evaluation, and most staff members have advanced degrees in quantitative fields, including operations research, statistics, and economics. Most of the group's staff came to Merck from analytical roles in other companies spanning numerous industries, including consulting, large pharmaceutical firms, health services research, physician licensure, insurance, and consumer packaged goods. In addition, the group maintains close partnerships with a variety of external providers of data and analytical software and services.

The Commercial Analytics group has been involved in a variety of key decisions at Merck over the last several years. When Merck re-engineered its commercial model for U.S. sales, the group piloted the model before it was adopted with test and control groups. Other work has quantified the impact and profitability of virtually all major investments in the physician and consumer channels. The group has also created tools for optimizing sales force sizes and structures along with multichannel programs.

Decision-Maker Partnerships

The Commercial Analytics group maintains a close set of relationships with internal business decision-makers. They have very positive comments about the group's role. One executive, responsible for strategy execution, commented:

> A lot of times Commercial Analytics team members were my "thought partners" in implementing the new field organization. Working with them was a good way of thinking something through. We used them as sounding boards. They are very solid problem solvers and play the role of an objective third party.

The same executive said that the Commercial Analytics team was more useful than an external resource that did similar types of work:

> Most of the other firms who did these new commercial models used an external consulting firm. We used them for some tasks, but we had our own algorithms developed by Commercial Analytics. They also found ways to optimize and test the pilots. It gave us a better result, as well as more internal buy-in.

The leader of a new business area that worked with Commercial Analytics also had positive comments about the value of the group's work and their credibility:

> Our business area is a pilot program. We want to show that it drives new revenue and provides better customer support. Commercial Analytics is measuring the impact of the pilot program. They set up a rigorous test-and-control approach... Commercial Analytics is very familiar with the business. They ask what business questions you are trying to answer, and then they identify how to measure them. They will analyze the data to see if they can answer the questions. Their level of

objectivity is what you need to have; we need an independent source... At times in the past, Commercial Analytics had to tell senior management that their project doesn't have good ROI. They are very credible when they do that. And if they say it works, there won't be any doubt about it.

A senior executive at Merck with global responsibilities emphasized the value of having Commercial Analytics involved in the entire decision process:

They should always be at the table when we are making an important decision. I remember when we were evaluating the returns on a major promotional campaign a while back. Commercial Analytics was at the table with us throughout the discussion and would engage with us in debate. Then they would do analysis to answer key questions. Having them be part of the team is a real competitive advantage for us.

Reasons for the Group's Success

There are undoubtedly many reasons why the Commercial Analytics and Decision Sciences group at Merck has been effective. The members of the group certainly have a high level of analytical skills, for example. Another key factor, however, is clearly the culture and relationships orientation in the group. The leadership team of Commercial Analytics emphasizes the key value of the organization:

The umbrella over everything we do is a culture of motivating team members with the prize that we are here to help our clients make better decisions through the use of our analytic insights and tools. Our rules of engagement are to make your internal client understand that you are there to help them make a better business decision.

The cultural orientation begins with clarity about the organization's mission and responsibilities. The group leader notes:

We're always objective about our findings. In a way we are the "Switzerland" of marketing and sales at Merck, providing a neutral perspective on those decisions. We work for the shareholders.

The group leader gives an example of how the group's independence affects its work with internal clients:

A lot of times managers will hear that we can do ROI analysis on promotions. So they come to me and ask if we can help them. I say, "We can do that, but let me ask you a question first. We will find that your promotion was very effective, marginally effective, or ineffective. Can you tell me what actions you'll take in each of those cases?" We document their answers and how the analytics will tie to them.

The Commercial Analytics' leadership team refuses to have the group engaged in a project if there is no clear relationship between an analysis and the decision to be made.

The group's strategy execution client confirms this approach:

Commercial Analytics always has the question of "How's this going to add value to our business?" at the front of their minds. They aren't chasing stuff as an academic exercise; they do a good job of checking to make sure that what they are about to tackle has business value. They ask, "What are you trying to get at? Maybe there is a better way to get there." I don't think it bothers anyone when they push back a little—they do it in a nice way.

One of the reasons that the group can work successfully with business decision-makers is its emphasis on clear and nontechnical communication about its work. Many of the analyses it undertakes are technically complex, but the Commercial Analytics leadership team devotes considerable effort to translating them into straightforward business terms. The group's leader describes this process:

We work hard at packaging our results in a way that is very intuitive and easy to digest for our business clients. If an analysis is not understandable to our client, then we failed to provide the appropriate graph, chart, or table. We do not avoid complex methods, but we make sure we can explain them.

One of our passions is distilling very complex ideas into simple terms so that business people can understand and apply them.

The executives at Merck we interviewed confirmed that the communications approaches are succeeding. For example, the executive leading the new business area noted:

Commercial Analytics communicates clearly to businesspeople. They were able to share their methodology with the marketing leaders whose products we are going to be selling. Since those managers are charged with sales force expense, they need to understand and evaluate our pilot.

The strategy execution executive described the communications ability of Commercial Analytics staff in similar terms:

The members of Commercial Analytics didn't come up through the sales area like I did, but they know they have to translate their findings into something that is "field-friendly." I know the folks in Commercial Analytics are always thinking about how to do that translation. I have worked with analytical people who are much more academic. It is more effective to work with Commercial Analytics.

Embedding Analyses into Tools

One other approach to improving decisions that the Commercial Analytics and Decision Sciences organization takes is to embed results into small software tools for use by marketing and sales managers in the field. The goal is to help field managers make better decisions by providing decision logic and data for the analyses they typically perform.

The group created a "channel choice simulation tool." It allows the user—typically the planner of a marketing campaign—to simulate the decision of channel selection for a particular product. The user can play with a variety of scenarios while attempting to optimize the returns on investments across channels. The output of the simulation is a probability of achieving a certain ROI level for a particular product.

Perhaps the most focused analysis tool is one for sales force vacancy management. If a sales rep leaves a particular region, should the manager fill the vacancy? This tool provides qualitative and quantitative analysis to inform the vacancy-filling decision. In a sense, it's a semiautomated checklist of the factors to consider in filling a sales vacancy. A sales manager's intuitive feeling about the need for a replacement is a key variable in the analysis.

Future Directions for Commercial Analytics and Decision Sciences

The leader of Commercial Analytics and the interviewed clients all feel that the group is providing considerable value for Merck. The key question going forward involves the direction for role expansion. Should Commercial Analytics, for example, expand beyond the U.S. market and provide support for global sales and marketing decisions? Business across Merck has become considerably more global through both acquisitions and organic growth, and the non-U.S. businesses need more analytical help with sales and marketing decisions. The downside, however, would be the possibility of providing too little support for important decisions in the U.S., which is the largest market at Merck.

Another option for role expansion would involve more "horizontal" collaboration with other analytics groups across Merck. In addition to Commercial Analytics, Merck has strong analytical capabilities in the R&D/clinical area, as well as in health economics and manufacturing. Thus far, the collaborations among these groups have been relatively minimal. Leadership of Commercial Analytics is aware that some other organizations, both within and outside of the pharmaceutical industry, are beginning to view analytics as more of an enterprise-level capability. Thus far, however, the specific benefits of greater collaboration are unclear.

Whatever the future roles of the Commercial Analytics and Decision Sciences organization, the values of independence, clear communications, and assistance to business decision-makers in multiple forms will continue. These cultural attributes are an important component of the group's success. They have led to a clear competitive advantage for Merck overall and for the executives who have taken advantage of the group's abilities.

18

Descriptive Analytics for the Supply Chain at Bernard Chaus, Inc.

Katherine Busey and Callie Youssi

In the midst of a severe economic downturn, Bernard Chaus, Inc., a women's apparel manufacturer, invested in a new business intelligence tool and database. They were designed to deliver descriptive analytics on supply chain performance. The tool was delivered "in the cloud" to company staff on a self-service basis. In just a matter of weeks, the firm had improved visibility throughout its supply chain, with almost immediate payback in the form of significant cost savings and closer customer relationships. Key to the successful implementation was extensive prior consultation with business unit leaders, who outlined the required data and functionality.

About Bernard Chaus, Inc.

The firm designs and sells upscale women's career and casual sportswear, primarily under the Josephine Chaus, Chaus, and Cynthia Steffe trademarks. Bernard Chaus's clothing is sold in about 4,000 U.S. department and specialty stores and is manufactured mostly in Asia. The company also manufactures private-label apparel and holds an exclusive license to make and sell the Kenneth Cole New York clothing lines. *(Source: Hoover's)*

Revenues: $110–120 million

Industry: Women's Apparel

CIO: Ed Eskew

Employees: 120
- IT: 5
- Analytics: 2 in-house

Technical infrastructure:
- RLM (apparel-focused ERP system)
- IBM AS400 servers
- IBM Rational development platform
- SKYPAD business intelligence tool
- QlikView analytics database

The Need for Supply Chain Visibility

As consumers reined in their spending during the financial crisis of 2008, apparel retailers struggled to control inventory, manage discounting, and maintain margins. Retailers began to press suppliers such as Bernard Chaus to assume more responsibility for analyzing sales trends, recommending markdowns, and adjusting shipments to reflect this data.

Like most of its peers at this point, however, Chaus relied on simple weekly phone checks with buyers and factories to determine manufacturing and replenishment plans. But this information was far less detailed than needed—and even potentially misleading. A retail buyer might report that a particular dress style was selling well, for example, while the reality was that just one size (of six) in one color (of three) accounted for the bulk of the sales. Without the ability to drill down to the specific SKU, the manufacturer might produce and air-freight more of every style variant, rather than sending more of the one hot seller and recommending early markdowns on the slower-selling items.

"We knew something was wrong, but we didn't know exactly where." —Ed Eskew

Chaus required greater visibility in both supply chain directions: back to its factories and shippers and forward to its wholesalers and retail buyers—all of whom were investing in data warehouse and communications infrastructure. To stay competitive, Eskew realized that the firm had to invest in a structured, automated feed of time-sensitive production, freight, and sales data—something only software could handle—as well as a business intelligence toolkit to "slice and dice" that information in support of smarter decision-making.

Before selecting a software vendor, Chaus's CIO did his organizational homework. Eskew understood that providing more complete supply chain visibility meant that acquiring and channeling production and sales data in and out of the enterprise was now his key task. But rather than rushing to a purchase decision and unilaterally delivering it to his users, he followed three deliberate steps:

1. Understand the business, and build personal trust. Eskew turned first to his business unit presidents and their "worker bees" and asked them these questions:

   - What information do you need for improved supply chain visibility?
   - When do you need this data? From whom should it come?
   - In what format?
   - What data can you supply?
   - How do your cutting, prototyping, ordering, and shipping processes work now? How would better data impact them? Where could you trim costs based on deeper and more timely data? Is there a better way to do any of these things?
   - Can you suggest a vendor's solution? If so, why? What features are critical?

   Most important, Eskew was simultaneously building one-to-one trust throughout this research. Not only did he personally appreciate organizational processes at a more detailed level, but he also established greater confidence and credibility in his subsequent decision-making.

   "Unless you know exactly what's going on, you lose control—and that's expensive." —Ed Eskew

2. Obtain executive backing. Eskew had to ensure that the firm's other C-level executives were onboard. In some companies, convincing top management to invest in new technology during a recession is difficult or impossible. But Eskew, with a decade's tenure at Chaus, knew that his CEO and CFO were aware of the challenges facing the company—including those related to lack of adequate supply chain visibility. He also knew that they never shied away from tough decisions.

As Eskew made the case for analytics, they also learned how implementing a data-rich approach would affect decisions: Everything from seasonal sales forecasting to communications with factories in China would undergo a major shift. Like the divisional presidents, all senior executives agreed that Eskew should lead the software selection process and implementation rollout.

3. Set prioritized criteria for the solution. Any software buyer can quickly come up with many criteria—ease of use, training, accessibility, service, and more—but Eskew knew that these were his top selection filters:

- An ability to house and support historical data in an easily retrievable manner
- Low startup costs compared with competitors
- Experience in apparel, retail, or a similar industry

Only when a vendor passed these screens were other criteria even considered. For Eskew, the selection wasn't about the fastest servers or nice-to-have bells and whistles. Instead, his focus remained on providing accurate and timely information about point-of-sale, synchronized production scheduling, freight management, factor financing, and other vital business variables.

"We knew we had to streamline our way back to profitability."
—Ed Eskew

With organizational backing and solution criteria established, vendor selection and implementation progressed rapidly. Over a couple of weeks, Eskew was able to narrow down the field to two potential vendors, including SKYPAD, a retail analytics and business intelligence platform from Sky I.T. Group. Also, after being impressed by a conference demonstration from QlikView, Eskew learned that SKYPAD closely interfaces with QlikView's database back-end. SKYPAD also "scrubs" and normalizes the wide variety of data types that Chaus encounters across its supply chain, from Excel spreadsheets to EDI transactions to Visuality style-image email exchanges between supplier and retailer. After a bit more due diligence, the vendor decision was a quick and straightforward one.

In the fall of 2008, only three weeks after selecting SKYPAD and well in time for the spring 2009 retail season, Chaus had a "plain vanilla" but functional model that revealed which SKUs were selling (and not selling) in specific locations—an immediate improvement over the previous manual process.

Eskew decided to launch with a bare-bones implementation to start seeing results and to learn what worked in the organization. Since then, based on feedback and suggestions from users, he has gradually but continually added options, data interchange formats, and user interface enhancements.

Analytics Strengthened Alignment Between Chaus's IT and Business Units

Today, Chaus holds weekly business unit meetings where the focus is on identifying new drivers of cost reduction. In a time-sensitive, competitive business like Eskew's, the volume and content of data never stop changing, nor does the potential for learning from experience. Thanks to close collaboration with IT throughout the initial implementation process, Chaus's business units have embraced SKYPAD as their go-to tool for gaining visibility into sales trends, operational efficiencies, demand planning, and predictive what-if analysis.

Because they helped "spec" it, the user community understands what SKYPAD is and what it can do. They now come to Eskew and his team to "figure things out," so the trust pays continuing benefits.

Eskew credits analytics with dramatically boosting the company's linkage between IT and the business units. On a five-stage Strategic Alignment Maturity Model scale where 1 = initial/ad hoc, 2 = committed, 3 = established/focused, 4 = improved/managed, and 5 = optimized, Eskew estimates that Chaus has gone from a 2.5 level of maturity to more than 4.0 in just two years.

> "Our goal is to become ever more responsive to what these tools can tell us." —Ed Eskew

With the new data in hand, Chaus managers can now confidently assist retailers in properly timing their item markdowns, which minimizes their end-of-season inventory. In subsequent seasons, too, retail buyers have good reason to trust Chaus's order-level recommendations. (Some stores have even turned seasonal inventory management entirely over to vendors like Chaus.) Because Chaus increasingly uses data to extend lead times, less money is spent on expensive, last-minute air freight from China.

Chaus's analytics investment produced virtually instant payback. Although Eskew initially established metrics to measure the firm's ROI, the payback was so quick that he soon stopped counting. Chaus's ramp-up costs were approximately $15,000, and SKYPAD's hosting charges—which vary based on customization and service requests—total about $50,000 annually. In contrast, Eskew estimates that Chaus has already saved well in excess of $1 million in reduced markdowns, better sell-through, and freight costs. "I can't quantify the total value," he says.

Because SKYPAD lets customers choose either hosted service or in-house implementation, Eskew knew that he could start on a monthly "cloud" basis and decide later to bring everything in-house. However, his experience with SaaS has been so positive—not to mention the absence of any new hardware investment—that Chaus plans to stick with the hosted approach.

> "Information without action is overhead." —Ed Eskew

Index

A

A/B testing, 16

Accenture, center of excellence model, 207

Acquah, Victor, 78

actions based on decisions, 98

activity, engagement versus, 72

advertising results assessment, web data for, 66-68

airline reservation proprietary data example, 40-41

Amadeus, 41

analyst sandbox, 129

analysts

engaging, 180-181

    business knowledge of, 182

    centralized organizational model, 185-186

    defined roles for, 183

    maintaining skills of, 184

organizing, 157

    assessment over time, 176-177

    CAO (Chief Analytics Officer), 173

    consolidating groups, 168-169

    coordination methods for analysts, 163-165

    ecosystem, building, 175-176

    goals of organizational structure, 158-159

    importance of, 157-158

    organizational models for, 160-162

    organization's goals, 159-160

    refining organizational model, 169-172

    reporting structure, 174-175

    variables to consider, 165-168

qualities of, Sears Holdings Corp. (SHC) case study, 235-237

types of, 179-180

analytical applications, 129

analytical ecosystem, building, 175-176

analytical intelligence, as analyst quality, 236

analytical orientation, analyst organization, 168

analytics

big-data analytics, 2-4, 16-17

business analytics

    attributes of, 123

    business unit-driven, 126